Spotlight on the Victorians

Sandy Brownjohn

Hodder & Stoughton
A MEMBER OF THE HODDER HEADLINE GROUP

Acknowledgements

The publisher would like to thank the following for permission to use copyright illustrations:

Hulton Getty p.4 (top); Royal Archives p.4 (bottom), p.6; Mary Evans Picture Library p.18; Hulton Deutsch p.20, p.34, p.68, p.71; Reprinted by permission of The Executors of the Estate of C. L. Dodgson and of A. P. Watt Ltd, p.24; The Illustrated London News Picture Library, p.15; Punch library p.42; Dickens' House Museum p.65; Mander & Mitchenson Theatre Collection p.69, p.70; Opie Collection p.73, p.92 (top), p.96 (right).

Every effort has been made to contact the holders of copyright material but if any have been inadvertently overlooked, the publisher will be pleased to make the necessary alterations at the first opportunity.

Orders: please contact Bookpoint Ltd, 39 Milton Park, Abingdon, Oxon OX14 4TD. Telephone: (44) 01235 400414, Fax: (44) 01235 400454. Lines are open from 9.00–6.00, Monday to Saturday, with a 24 hour message answering service. Email address: orders@bookpoint.co.uk

British Library Cataloguing in Publication Data
A catalogue record for this title is available from The British Library

ISBN 0 340 69729 6

First published 1998

Impression number	10 9 8 7 6 5 4 3 2
Year	2004 2003 2002 2001 2000 1999 1998

Typeset by Mind's Eye Design.
Printed in Great Britain for Hodder & Stoughton Educational, a division of Hodder Headline Plc, 338 Euston Road, London NW1 3BH by Scotprint Ltd, Mussleburgh, Scotland.

Contents

page

The reign of Queen Victoria 4
Victorian eponyms 8
The Empire 10
Victoria's language legacy 12
Understanding Victorian money 15
Marriage 18
Household hints 21
Victorian parlour games 22
Life in the countryside 25
Schools 28
Working children 34
Public health 37
Police and detection 40
Slang 44
Popular word games 49
Poets 52
Lewis Carroll and his word games 55
Victorian light verse 58
Parodies 62
The satire of Dickens, Thackeray and Trollope 65
Theatres and dream palaces 68
Victorian toys 72
Children's books 76
More Victorian parlour games 81
Letters 84
Horror and the supernatural 86
Magazines 89
Newspapers 92
Advertising 94

The reign of Queen Victoria

In this extract from her diary, Princess Victoria describes how she learnt that her uncle King William IV, had died and she was now Queen:

20 June, 1837

I was awoke at 6 o'clock by Mama ... I got out of bed and went into my sitting room (only in my dressing-gown), and alone, and saw them. Lord Conyngham (the Lord Chamberlain) then acquainted me that my poor Uncle, the King, was no more, ... and consequently that I am Queen ... I shall do my utmost to fulfil my duty towards my country; I am very young and perhaps in many, though not all things, inexperienced. But I am sure, that very few have more real good will and more real desire to do what is fit and right than I have.

Queen Victoria.

So began the reign of Queen Victoria which lasted a record 64 years until her death in 1901. No other British King or Queen has reigned so long.

During her reign she saw great advances in medicine, science and engineering. The industrial revolution meant that Britain led the world in manufacturing and this produced a growing wealthy middle class which gradually became important in all areas of public life. It was a time of expansion overseas when the British Empire grew to be the greatest ever seen in the history of the world. Literature and the arts flourished and writers, such as Charles Dickens and Thomas Hardy, captured these changing times in novels which are still important to us today.

It was also an era of great poverty and social need which gave rise to reformers like Lord Shaftesbury, Dr Barnardo and Octavia Hill. The Education Act of 1870 heralded the beginning of education for everyone. This, along with the rise of unions and the demand for extending the vote to the working classes and women, ensured that by the end of Victoria's reign Britain would never be quite the same again.

Victoria's Diary

Throughout her life Queen Victoria kept a diary. Read the following extracts in which she describes the most important personal experiences during her long reign.

28 June 1938

[on her coronation day] . . . *It was a fine day, and the crowds of people exceeded what I have ever seen; ... millions of my loyal subjects were assembled in every spot to witness the Procession. Their good-humour and excessive loyalty was beyond everything, and I really cannot say how proud I feel to be the Queen of such a Nation ... I re-entered my carriage, the Crown on my head and Sceptre and Orb in my hand . . . I shall remember this day as the proudest of my life.*

15 October 1839

. . . I sent for Albert . . . I said to him, that I thought he must be aware why I wished [him] to come here – and that it would make me too happy if he would consent to what I wished (to marry me). I told him I was quite unworthy of him – he said he would be very happy 'das Leben mit dir zu zubringen' ['to spend my life with you'], *and was so kind and seemed so happy, that I really felt it was the happiest brightest moment in my life.*

11 February 1840

[the morning after Victoria and Albert's wedding] *When day dawned (for we did not sleep much) and I beheld that beautiful angelic face by my side, it was more than I can express! He does look so beautiful in his shirt only, with his beautiful throat seen. . . . At 12 I walked out with my precious Angel, all alone – so delightful, on the Terrace and new Walk, arm in arm!*

The marriage was extremely happy and both were devoted to each other. Albert took a keen interest in all matters of state and Victoria relied on his advice and judgement in all things. They had nine children.

The Death of Albert

13 December 1861

Found him very quiet and comfortably warm, and so dear and kind, called me 'gutes Fräuchen' [good little wife] *and kissed me so affectionately and so completely like himself, and I held his dear hands between mine ... They gave him brandy every half-hour.*

14 December 1861

Never can I forget how beautiful my darling looked lying there with his face lit up by the rising sun ... I took his dear left hand which was already cold ... Two or three long but perfectly gentle breaths were drawn, the hand clasping mine and ... all, all, was over ... I stood up, kissed his dear heavenly forehead and called out in a bitter and agonizing cry, 'Oh! my dear Darling!'

21 August 1862

[at Balmoral, at the top of Craig Lowrigan] *The view was so fine, the day so bright, and the heather so beautifully pink – but no pleasure, no joy! all dead!*

And here at the top is the foundation of the cairn – forty feet wide – to be erected to my precious Albert, ... I and my poor six orphans all placed stones on it, and our initials, as well as those of the three absent ones, are to be carved on stones all round it. I felt very shaky and nervous.

It is to be thirty-five feet high, and the following inscription to be placed on it:

TO THE BELOVED MEMORY
OF
ALBERT, THE GREAT AND GOOD
PRINCE CONSORT
RAISED BY HIS BROKEN-HEARTED WIDOW
VICTORIA R.
AUGUST 21, 1862

'He being made perfect in a short time fulfilled a long time;
For his soul pleased the Lord,
Therefore hastened He to take him
Away from among the wicked.'

Wisdom of Solomon, iv. 13, 14

Does anything surprise you about the extracts from Queen Victoria's diaries? Do you think she wrote them for other people to read or just for herself?

Write a diary for a week. Imagine your diary is your best friend and write as you would speak to him or her. Write something every day and record how you feel and what you think about people and events.

Then imagine that your headteacher or a parent has asked to see your diary – choose two days from your diary and rewrite them in a more formal way. Now compare your diary entries – in what ways have they changed? Did you write things differently or even miss bits out?

Look for other examples of Victorian *epitaphs*, like the one Queen Victoria had inscribed for Prince Albert. (An epitaph is an inscription, sometimes in verse, which is put on a grave or tomb, and you can usually find examples in old churchyards. It can also be something written on the occasion of someone's death. It commemorates the person's life and helps to remind us of them.)

You could also try writing an epitaph in verse for someone from the past, now dead. It could be for someone you knew, or someone you have read about.

This epitaph is in the churchyard of St Nicholas, Great Yarmouth. (Notice the spelling of 'angel'.)

Victorian eponyms

An *eponym* is a new word that comes from someone's name. It can describe the personality or sort of behaviour for which that person is famous. Eponyms can derive from real or fictional characters, and even animals. Objects can also be named after people. Here are a few Victorian eponyms:

Batty means to be harmlessly insane, or dotty. The word comes from a barrister called Fitzherbert Batty who lived in Spanish Town, Jamaica. In 1839 his odd behaviour resulted in his being certified insane and this was widely reported in the London newspapers, catching the public's imagination.

Bob's Your Uncle means something that is easy to achieve. The expression dates back to 1887 when the Prime Minister was Robert (Bob) Cecil, Lord Salisbury. When needing to appoint someone to the important government post of Chief Secretary for Ireland, he chose to give it to his nephew, Arthur Balfour. Up to that point Balfour had not shown any particular abilities, and people thought that he only got the job because of his uncle.

Boycott means to refuse to have anything to do with someone or something. In 1880, Captain Charles Cunningham Boycott was acting as an estate manager and agent in Mayo, Ireland. He evicted several tenants who could not afford higher rents, and then took over their land. Charles Parnell, president of the Irish Land League which protected tenant workers, encouraged people to shun him in every way. Unable to buy or sell any goods, Boycott was forced to leave Ireland. The method became known as 'boycotting' and was used against others.

Crap means useless rubbish or waste; and, also, to go to the toilet. Both these meanings are thought to come from the name of the inventor of the first flush lavatory sold in England. Thomas Crapper called his invention *Crapper's Valveless Water Waste Preventer*.

Plimsoll line and plimsolls – When the water reaches the horizontal line on the side of a ship it shows that the maximum load is on board. This line is called the Plimsoll line, after Samuel Plimsoll who worked hard to get the Merchant Shipping Act through parliament in 1876. After this date, many fewer ships sank and Plimsoll became a hero to ordinary seamen. The rubber-soled gym shoes also take his name, probably because the top of the rubber rim on the shoe looks like a Plimsoll line.

Trilby – A trilby is a soft felt hat, with a ridge on the top. The name comes from the heroine of George du Maurier's novel *Trilby* published in 1894. A play based on the novel was staged in London in 1895 and the hats were worn in this production.

Match these Victorian eponyms to their meanings.

A woolly garment for keeping warm	**Everest**
A large bell that keeps time	**Big Ben**
A very high mountain	**Cardigan**
Fair rules for boxing	**Jekyll and Hyde**
Someone who leads a double life, or a personality with a good and a bad side	**Queensberry Rules**

Then find out the history of each eponym and write it down. (You could start your own 'Dictionary of Eponyms' and add to it as you come across new ones).

The British Empire 'on which the Sun never sets'

It was during Victoria's reign that Britain's Empire grew to be the largest in the world. It was called 'the Empire on which the Sun never sets' because it stretched all over the globe and at any time of day or night the sun would be shining on one or other of its lands.

The extent of the British Empire by 1900.

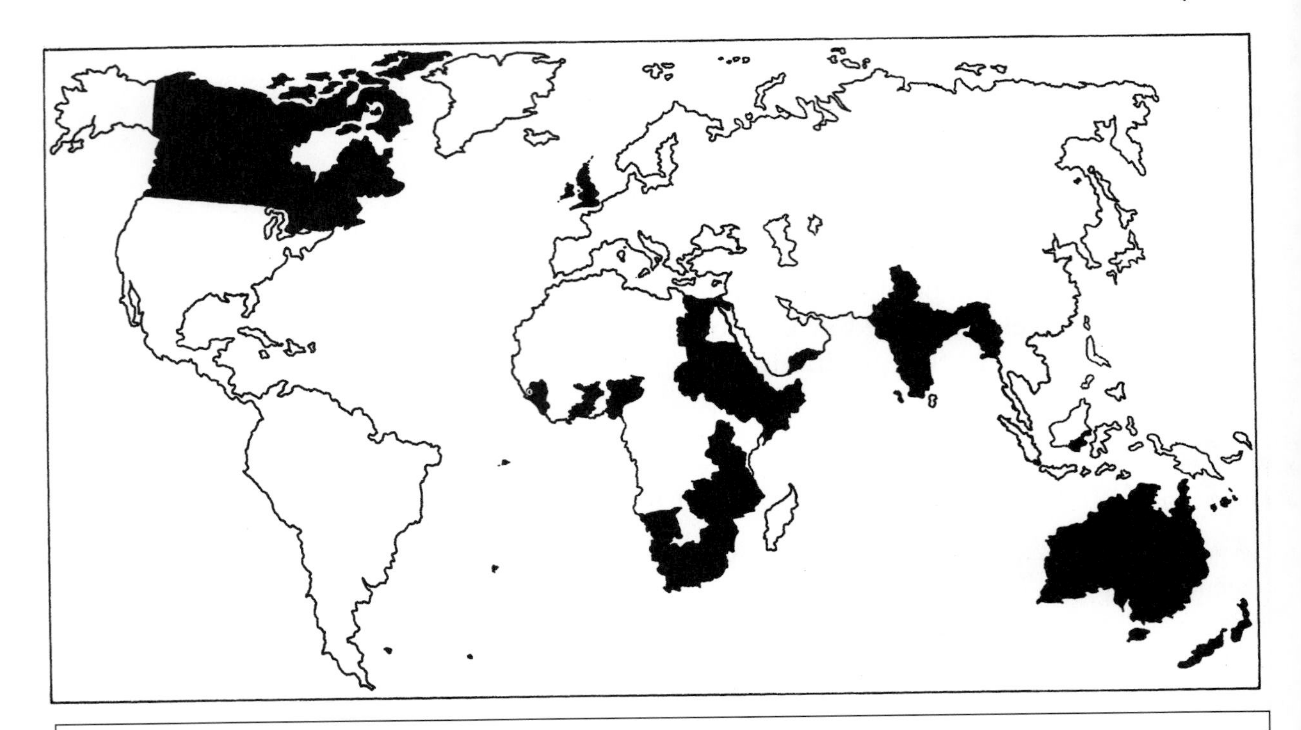

The present population of the British Empire is now said to exceed three hundred and nine millions. And what a golden round of sovereignty shines in those figures. There are the dusky myriads of British India and Ceylon; the peoples of British North America, of Australasia, and South Africa, our dark fellow subjects of the Gold Coast, the West Indies, Honduras, the Straits, Guiana, Fiji and Borneo; there are tattooed Maoris and British blended in New Zealand, pig-tailed Chinese and British at Hong Kong, yellow-robed Buddhists and British in Burma. Those figures carry the mind from the white rocks of Malta to the black crags of Perim and Aden; over vast seas dotted with the stations of the Queen's flag; over expanses so studded with colonies …

From the *Daily Telegraph,* 1887

The reasons for the Empire

In simple terms, the main reason for Britain building up its Empire was for it to become richer and more powerful. Ownership of new lands meant that Britain could make money from natural resources it did not have at home, such as diamonds, gold, rubber and spices. It also meant that there were new markets in which to sell goods manufactured at home. Spain, France, Italy, Germany, Holland and Portugal were also building empires for the same reasons.

Borrowed words

The English language is basically Anglo-Saxon. However, for centuries, words from all over the world have entered the language and become part of its vocabulary.

Find out where these words came from originally. A good dictionary, or, better still, a dictionary of English Etymology, which gives word origins, will help you.

bamboo banana bangle boomerang bungalow cannibal chimpanzee chutney
cocoa coffee curry dinghy jungle kangaroo ketchup kiwi koala launch
moccasin moose pow-wow shampoo taboo tattoo thug tomahawk verandah

During the nineteenth century, more new words found their way into English from all over the world, particularly from parts of the Empire. Here are some words that appeared in English for the first time while Victoria was on the throne:

– alfalfa, loofah, safari, yashmak – gymkhana, juggernaut, khaki, loot, polo, pyjamas – hara-kiri, samurai, tycoon – chipmunk, igloo, tepee – tsetse, voodoo – raffia – commandeer, dope, trek – bonanza, canyon, cigarette, coyote – budgerigar.

Find out what they mean and where they originally came from. The words are grouped according to their places of origin.

Trace the outline only of a map of the world on to a piece of paper. Now, on your outline map, write all the borrowed words on this page into the parts of the world where they originated.

Victoria's language legacy

Both Victoria and her husband, Albert, the Prince Consort, were honoured during the reign by people naming things after them.

A VICTORIA SANDWICH *is a sponge cake of two layers filled with jam.*

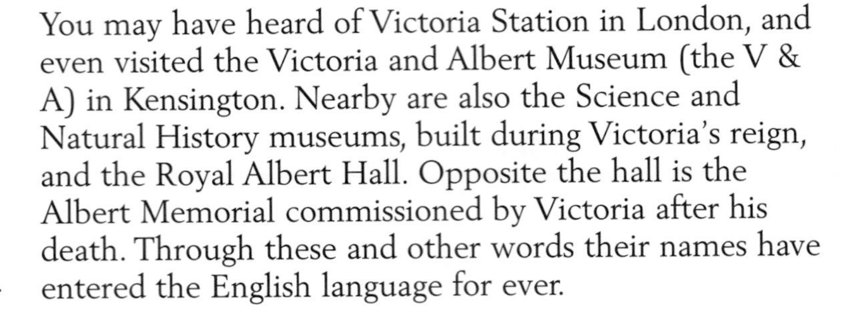

You may have heard of Victoria Station in London, and even visited the Victoria and Albert Museum (the V & A) in Kensington. Nearby are also the Science and Natural History museums, built during Victoria's reign, and the Royal Albert Hall. Opposite the hall is the Albert Memorial commissioned by Victoria after his death. Through these and other words their names have entered the English language for ever.

Victorian values

VICTORIAN VALUES is a phrase that politicians often use today. They are held up to be the right way of leading a good life. They reflect the values of the middle classes of Victorian times and stand for decency, harmony, thrift, family security, hard work, discipline and order. The well off looked down on 'the undeserving poor' who did not follow these values. However, as you will see, many middle class people failed to live by these values and the poor had very little chance to do so as they lived in such desperate poverty.

The VICTORIA CROSS, *created in 1856, is inscribed 'For Valour' and is awarded 'for bravery in the presence of the enemy.' It is Britain's highest military and naval medal and was originally made from the metal of Russian guns captured in the Crimean War.*

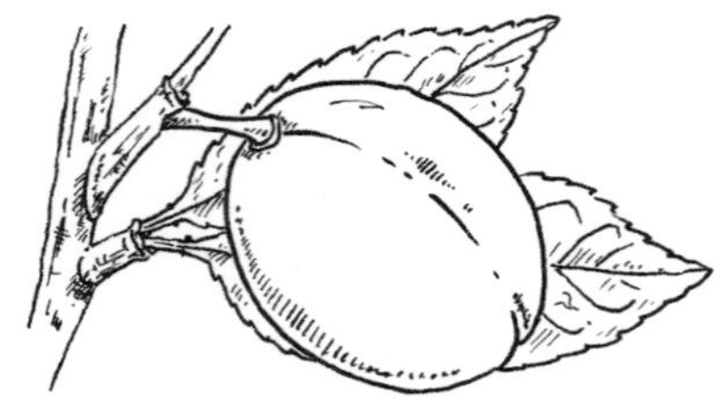

The VICTORIA PLUM, *first named in 1860, is a tasty fruit with a rich red colour.*

An ALBERT, *was a watch chain which stretched across a waistcoat from one pocket to another. Prince Albert set the fashion in 1849 after receiving a chain as a gift.*

Victorian place names

The Empire

All over the world explorers and Empire-builders honoured their Queen by naming places after her or her husband. For example, the Victoria Falls in Africa and Alberta in Canada.

> ? Find a modern atlas and look up other places that were named after Victoria and Albert. In which countries do you find the most?
>
> Now look at the map of the British Empire on page 10. What do you notice?

Street names

Before 1800 most people lived and worked in the country. By 1851, due to the industrial revolution, half the population lived in cities and towns and by 1900 this had risen to three quarters. Towns and cities grew fast as the new factories needed more workers.

Acacia

Those who could afford it often moved out to the edges of towns where life was more pleasant and the housing was better. Many of these suburbs had streets named after flowers and trees, often the new exotic varieties that were being brought to Britain from all over the Empire. Some favourite street names include Acacia, Laburnum, Juniper, Jasmine and Cedar.

Juniper

Other streets were often named after famous people. As well as the royal family, almost all well-known Victorians from all walks of life have been commemorated in this way.

Jasmine

Look at a street map of your nearest town to see how many famous Victorian names you can find. The following selection will help you. Can you find any of them on your map?

Royalty

Queen Victoria, Victoria, Albert, Prince Albert, Prince Consort, Regent, Prince George, Princess May.

Statesmen

Cecil (Salisbury), Peel, Palmerston, Melbourne, Gladstone, Balfour, Disraeli (Beaconsfield), Plimsoll, Shaftesbury, Rosebery, Lansdowne, Keir Hardie.

Explorers, Empire-Builders and Defenders

Cardigan, Rhodes, Stanley, Livingstone, Gordon, Florence Nightingale, (Mary) Seacole, Speke, Baden-Powell.

Writers, Artists, Actors and Musicians

Tennyson, Browning, Dickens, Thackeray, Kipling, Wordsworth, Kingsley, Brontë, Wilde, Whistler, Turner, Landseer, Kemble, Irving, Elgar, Hallé.

Scientists and Engineers

Darwin, Lister, Faraday, Isambard (Kingdom) Brunel, Marconi, Dunlop.

Look also for streets named after royal palaces, national events or important places in the Empire, often scenes of battles.

Royal Palaces

Windsor, Sandringham (bought in 1861), Balmoral (bought in 1848), Osborne (House, Isle of Wight, bought in 1845 and Victoria's favourite residence).

National Events

Coronation, Jubilee.

Empire

Mafeking, Kimberley, Rhodesia, Ladysmith.

Find out about some of the people whose names are on streets in *your* area. (Encyclopaedias and your local library will help you in the first instance and also some of them are featured in this book.)

This street in London is named after Rowland Hill, who introduced the Penny Black postage stamp.

Understanding Victorian money

The Victorians used the imperial system of currency – we use the decimal system today. In imperial money there were 12 pennies (12d) in a shilling and twenty shillings (20s or 20/-) in a sovereign or pound.

Some coins

Sovereign (£1)
Crown (5s or 5/-)
Half Crown (2s 6d, 2/6)
Shilling (1s, 1/-)
Sixpence (6d)
Twopenny piece (2d)
Penny (1d)
Farthing (1/4d)

Making sense of prices

Because the value of money changes, it is often difficult to compare prices with our own times. The best way to begin to understand is to look at the costs of items then and now. Some things seem to have increased in price much more than others.

? Find out what the nearest equivalent of the following would cost today. Then try to work out roughly what each of the above coins would be worth in today's money.

In 1870 a football kit cost	
Jersey	*1/10 or 1s 10d*
Shorts	*2/- or 2s*
Boots	*5/11 or 5s 11d*
Ball	*6/6 or 6s 6d*

In the 1880s and 1890s	
A haircut	*2d*
Butter	*1/3 (1s 3d) per lb*
Tea	*4/- (4s) per lb*
New Zealand Lamb	*$7\frac{1}{2}$d per lb*
Sugar	*2d per lb*
Potatoes	*$\frac{1}{2}$d per lb*
Cheese	*$7\frac{1}{4}$d per lb*
The latest Penny Farthing Bicycle with gears	*£12*

Factory worker – 'I work ten hours a day, six days a week in a factory. I earn about £32 a year.'

Servant girl – 'I work as a servant girl in a large house. I get board and lodging and about £8 a year in wages.'

Carpenter – 'I'm a carpenter and I earn about £71 a year.'

BUILDING COSTS

A gentleman's country house *£2,000*

A farm labourer's cottage
(2 rooms up, 2 down and an outside privy) *£150*

Renting a new mansion block flat
(4 rooms) *4/- (4s) per week*

Wages

How people live depends largely on how much they earn. In 1873, out of a population of 31 million, a mere 7,000 people owned four-fifths of the land in the United Kingdom. Their estates gave them at least £3,000 per year, and usually more – much more in the case of the Duke of Bedford who received £244,000 that year!

However, 75 per cent of the population had to work for a living. For middle class families to keep up a household with two servants (a maid and a nursemaid) it cost around £300 a year. Of course, most people earned much less:

Come all you bold Britons where'er you may be,
I pray give attention and listen to me.
There once was good times, but they're gone by complete,
For a man lives now on eight shillings a week.

Such times in old England there never was seen,
As the present ones now, but much better have been.
A poor man's condemned and considered a thief,
And compelled to work hard on eight shillings a week.

The Nobs of Old England, of shameful renown,
Are striving to crush a poor man to the ground.
They'll beat down their wages and starve them complete,
And make them work hard for eight shillings a week....

(Excerpt from a well-known folk song about farm labourers of the 1840s)

The poor

Many people had little or no money and there were thousands of men, women and children living in poverty, either in terrible slum conditions or on the streets. Every town and city had beggars as well as street criminals. Charles Dickens' novel, Oliver Twist, gives a vivid picture of life in the workhouse, the London streets and the rookeries, which were the warren-like buildings inhabited by hundreds of petty criminals.

Here is one farmworker's family's income and expenditure for a week. The older children also work on the farm, probably as birdscarers (they would work in the fields, keeping the birds away from the crops). Notice their ages.

INCOME		EXPENDITURE			
Father (42yrs)	*9s a week*	Bread	*9s*	Thread etc	*2d*
Mother (40)	*9d*	Potatoes	*1s*	Candles	*3d*
Boy (12)	*2s*	Rent	*1s 2d*	Salt	*½d*
Boy (11)	*1s*	Tea	*2d*	Coal/wood	*9d*
Boy (8)	*1s*	Sugar	*3½d*	Butter	*4½d*
2 children (6 & 4) not working		Soap	*3d*	Cheese	*3d*
		Blue	*½d*		
TOTAL	***13s 9d***			TOTAL	***13s 9d***

Write down a typical weekly shopping list for your family and compare it with that of the farm labourer's family above. What do you notice about the two lists? What does it tell you about the way a farmworker's family lived?

Look carefully at the folk song on page 16. What does it tell you about the mood of the farm labourer? Why is he angry?

Imagine you are a young birdscarer on a big estate, owned by a rich Duke. Make up a folk song describing your hard life – remember you may never have been to school, you work long hours in all weather, you may be cruelly treated, you are often hungry …

● ● ● ● ● ●

Marriage

Mama's birthday, 1871.

Six Rules For A Perfect Marriage

1. Be the Perfect Man or Woman
2. Be the Perfect Gentleman or Lady
3. Share Purses and ALL Interests Together
4. Improve and Be Improved By Each Other
5. Promote Each Other's Happiness
6. Redouble Love by Redeclaring it

(Professor Fowler, 1883)

The Victorians believed strongly in marriage and families. The woman stayed at home, looking after the children, sewing, cooking and making sure that her husband was comfortable after work. Better off families had servants, and wives could spend their time learning a musical instrument, practising singing or improving their embroidery skills.

For the poor, married life was very different. Mothers struggled to feed their children and often had to work long hours for very little pay. Many unmarried mothers died in childbirth in grim workhouses, like Fanny Robin in Thomas Hardy's *Far From The Madding Crowd*, or the mother of Charles Dickens' *Oliver Twist*. Many men treated their wives as mere possessions as does Michael Henchard in Thomas Hardy's *The Mayor of Casterbridge*.

'For my part I don't see why men who have got wives and don't want 'em, shouldn't get rid of 'em as these gypsy fellows do their old horses. Why shouldn't they put 'em up and sell 'em by auction to men who are in need of such articles? Hey? Why, begad, I'd sell mine this minute if anybody would buy her!'

The ideal wife

'As a general rule, it is highly desirable that ladies should keep their temper; a woman when she storms always makes herself ugly, and usually ridiculous also … no man ever wished to have his wife remarkable for forward prowess than retiring gentleness. A low voice is an excellent thing in woman'.

(Anthony Trollope, *Barchester Towers*)

'She thinks it no degradation that she should take pains to please, to soothe, to comfort the man who all day long has been doing irksome work ... her womanliness inclines her to loving forbearance, to patience under difficulties, to unwearied cheerfulness ... she understands that she must take the rough with the smooth; but that, as her husband's way of life is rougher than hers, his trials greater, his burden heavier, it is her duty – and her privilege – to help him all she can with her tenderness and her love.'

(Elizabeth Lynn Linton)

Women who did not marry were generally pitied and a young woman would spend much of her time trying to attract a suitable husband. In 1879 Jeanette Marshall, 21 years old, recorded in her diary her attempts to find a husband –

Mr Brown is really very pleasing. Still, he may come once and never again.

Papa is concerned about Mr Brown, and thinks there must be a reason for his silence. I begin to forget him. I can't help feeling that he did care for me. However, it is all past and gone and I shall never marry now.

It has been a horrid year. Mr Brown has vanished utterly, A.D. only seen once, for an instant. Mr Cartwright is also invisible again.

The ideal husband

The ideal Victorian middle-class husband was respectable, hard-working, considerate and protective of his wife and children. He might appear stern, but he also tried to be fair. In practice, many husbands found homelife so dull that they often went to gentlemen's clubs to meet male friends. Others found female company at theatres, music halls and pleasure gardens, places not considered respectable enough for their wives. It was quite usual for a devoted husband and caring father regularly to seek out the pleasures of prostitutes, before returning to his 'respectable' home.

The Gentlemen's Club

? Choose one of the following –

Re-read all the extracts in this section. Are there any which contain things that a person might write or think today? Which ones are they?

Discuss Victorian values and views on women and marriage, and compare them with those of today. What are the main differences and why do you think they have changed? Is life better now for everybody? Have some things *not* changed, and if not, why not? Should they have changed?

Look back at the 'Six rules for a perfect marriage' at the beginning of this section. Make up your own modern 'Six rules for a perfect relationship'.

Household hints

Household hints

These are some of the useful tips which were offered to the Victorian housewife.

IN PUTTING ON CHILDREN'S HOODS care should be taken that the ears lie in their natural position, flat, underneath them. If the hood is carelessly put on, the ears may easily be doubled forward by it, and become permanently deformed if the habit is continued. Children's ears are also frequently disfigured by hats which are pressed down too low upon the head, or by the elastics or strings of the hats, which, being carelessly passed under the chin, push the ears forwards and outwards.

A MID-DAY SLEEP is desirable in summer for all children under the age of nine, and they should sleep on the bed in a darkened room, with the window open. Draughts should be prevented by a screen placed round the bed, or curtains, for fresh air can do no harm, but draughts, even in summer, are always dangerous. Over-heating and fatigue must be avoided both before and after meals, for those that sit down to table exhausted by heat and exercise run considerable risk of indigestion.

FLATULENCE after meals is very disagreeable, and is a symptom, usually, of indigestion, produced, as often as not, by exertion being made too soon after eating. A simple remedy is five drops of pure terebene*, taken on a piece of sugar, which is to be allowed to dissolve in the mouth.

(* terebene was a disinfectant made from oil of turpentine)

GIRLS WHO SUFFER FROM PIMPLES find that watercress is an excellent blood-purifier, and it should be eaten daily with breakfast, it should, however, be very carefully washed before it is eaten. Watercress has a peculiar faculty of absorbing iron from the water in which it grows, and thus, if it is grown on a soil containing much iron, it is excellent for anaemic persons.

TO WATERPROOF A FELT HAT – Remove the lining, and paint the inside with Canada balsam made hot. Hats made waterproof and not ventilated will bring on premature baldness, so punch a few holes in the side.

Victorian parlour games

Riddles

People have enjoyed riddles for centuries. Victorians liked riddles which relied on wordplay and they were a favourite after-dinner and party entertainment. However, by the end of the era, they had gone out of fashion in polite society:

> 'Luckily for this generation, the tyranny of the English riddle is overpast. Familiarity with such a conversational kill-joy has long been reckoned the reverse of a social accomplishment.'
>
> (Chambers' Journal, 29 July 1893)

SOME VICTORIAN RIDDLES

What is the difference between a cat and a comma?
A cat has its claws at the end of its paws, and a comma has its pause at the end of its clause.

What is the difference between an engine-driver and a schoolmaster?
One minds the train, and the other trains the mind.

What is the difference between an elephant and a flea?
An elephant can have fleas but a flea can't have elephants.

What is the difference between a rhododendron and a cold apple-dumpling?
The one is a rhododendron and the other is a cold apple-dumpling!

Why is the letter T like Easter?
Because it comes at the end of Lent.

When is coffee like the soil?
When it is ground.

Why is a thought like the sea?
Because it's a notion (an ocean).

Why is the Desert of Arabia the best place for a picnic?
Because of the sand which is there.

Even Queen Victoria liked trying to solve riddles:

> 'Her Majesty takes delight in a clever riddle or rebus, but on one occasion she was very angry at having been hoaxed over a riddle which was sent to her with a letter to the effect that it had been made by the Bishop of Salisbury. For four days the Queen and Prince Albert sought for the reply, when Charles Murray (Controller of the Household) was directed to write to the bishop and ask for the solution. The answer received was that the bishop had not made the riddle nor could he solve it.'
>
> (from *The Private Life of the Queen* (1897) by 'One of Her Majesty's Servants'.)

Riddles survive today, particularly in joke books; and although these are aimed at children, many adults enjoy them too. The English language is very rich in puns, often based on homonyms or homophones.

Look at the riddles on the previous page to see how they work. Which of them fit the following categories?

Homonyms – words with the same spelling but different meanings

Homophones – words with the same sound but different spellings and meanings

Simple logic – it makes us laugh because it's so obvious

Spoonerism-type – initial letters, or even whole words, change places and make another meaning

Now compile your own Drawing-Room Amusements book of the sort popular with Victorians. Find examples in your own joke books of the kind of riddles on the opposite page (or you may know some already which you could use) and arrange them according to how they work (ie the different language techniques used). Illustrate the book to make it more fun.

Lewis Carroll put the following riddle into *Alice in Wonderland* but he had no answer for it. Many people wrote to him asking for the solution. Can you come up with a wordplay answer?

Why is a raven like a writing desk?

Rebuses

A Rebus is a puzzle that uses pictures, numbers or letters of the alphabet which form words or sentences when read aloud. For example:

B	
= *bone* (**B** on **E**)	
E	

I suspicion		
that		*I overheard that he's under suspicion*
heard he's		

I C U R the 1 4 me	I 8 PPP 4 T

This clever example comes from *Puzzles for Leisure Hours* (1876) by Thomas Owen.

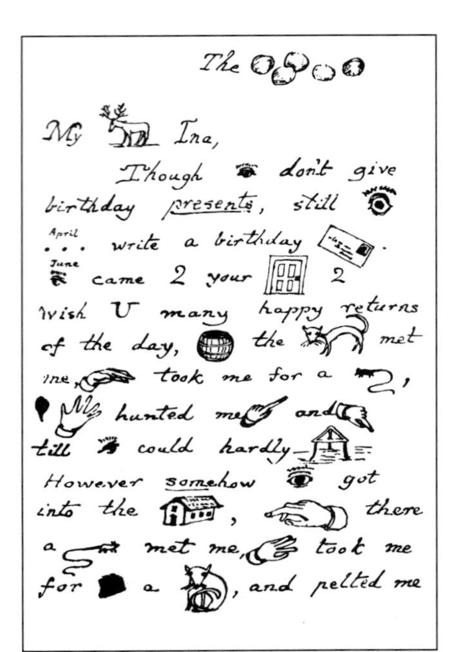
The

My Ina,

Though don't give birthday presents, still
April ... write a birthday .
June came 2 your 2
wish U many happy returns
of the day, the met
me, took me for a ,
hunted me and
till could hardly .
However somehow got
into the , there
a met me, took me
for a , and pelted me

rebellion rebellion
In 1789
FRA NCE
laws
monarchy
thrown
religion (printed upside down)
rebellion rebellion

(In 1789, France was divided, monarchy overthrown, laws set aside, religion turned upside down, with rebellion at every corner.)

People also enjoyed writing letters and puzzles using pictures to stand for words. Look at the letter on the left that Lewis Carroll wrote to Georgina Watson. It begins, 'My "deer" Ina.'

?

Write your own Rebus picture letter. You could write to Lewis Carroll about the *Alice* books, or even to one of the characters from them; for example, the Cheshire Cat, the Mad Hatter, or the White Rabbit.

Make up a Rebus using numbers and/or letters of the alphabet. It must make sense.

If you feel more ambitious, try a longer Rebus, like the one above about France.

Life in the countryside

> 'We labourers had no lack of lords and masters. There was the parson and his wife at the rectory. There was the squire, with his hand of iron over-shadowing us all. At the sight of the squire the people trembled. He lorded it right feudally over his tenants, the farmers; the farmers in their turn tyrannised over the labourers; the labourers were no better than toads under a harrow...
>
> [The farmers] impressed themselves on me as taskmasters and oppressors, and my heart used to burn within me when I heard of their doings, and when I saw how the men who toiled so hard for them were treated like the dirt beneath their feet.'

This extract is from the autobiography of Joseph Arch (1826–1919) who began life as a poor farm labourer. He went on to become a spokesman for his fellows, encouraging them to form a trade union and fight for better wages and conditions. In 1889 he became the first working class MP when he was elected to represent North-West Norfolk in parliament.

Life could be very hard and wages lower than in the towns. However, people in the country were often closer. Where families knew each other and had grown up together, they would help each other in difficult times. They also kept up the old traditions and enjoyed celebrating together on feast days and holidays. The writer who most captured what life was like then, was Thomas Hardy.

Thomas Hardy

Hardy grew up in rural Dorset. Although he qualified as an architect, he did not work at this for long. Instead, he began writing novels and short stories, set in the West Country which he called Wessex. His books show how life in the country was changing during the century, with the new machines which could do the work of many people:

> Close under the eaves of the stack ... was the red tyrant that the women had come to serve – a timber-framed construction with straps and wheels appertaining – the threshing machine which, whilst it was going, kept a despotic demand upon the endurance of their muscles and nerves.
>
> (from *Tess of the D'Urbervilles* by Thomas Hardy)

He also wrote about the drift away from the land to jobs in the industrial towns. He showed how hard life could be for the people who remained, and described the old ways and customs, many of which have since died out.

Customs

One custom was the Hiring or Mop Fair which was generally held around Michaelmas Day (29 September), or occasionally in the spring. Labourers needing work would stand in the market holding a symbol of the job they were after. Farmers would pick those they wanted and take them on for the next year. To seal the contract a worker was given 'earnest money', usually a shilling.

> ? When reading the passage below, consider the following: why do you think the farmers shied away from Gabriel when they learned that he had once had his own farm?
>
> What do you think of this way of hiring labour?

Gabriel Oak, who has lost his own sheep farm, looks for a job:

> At one end of the street stood from two to three hundred blithe and hearty labourers waiting upon Chance... Among these, carters and waggoners were distinguished by having a piece of whip-cord twisted round their hats; thatchers wore a fragment of woven straw; shepherds held their sheep-crooks in their hands; and thus the situation required was known to the hirers at a glance...
>
> [Gabriel] stood on the kerb of the pavement, as a shepherd, crook in hand. Now that Oak had turned himself into a shepherd it seemed that bailiffs were most in demand. However, two or three farmers noticed him and drew near...
>
> *'Whose farm were you upon last?'*
>
> *'My own.'*
>
> This reply invariably operated like a rumour of cholera. The inquiring farmer would edge away and shake his head dubiously.
>
> (from *Far From The Madding Crowd* by Thomas Hardy)

Another custom was the traditional Mummers' Play. The main characters were St George, the dragon, a giant and a Turkish Knight. Once it was usual for men of a village to perform it as entertainment at Christmas. Nowadays the tradition is only practised in a very few places, either at Christmas or at Easter.

'Ah, the mummers, the mummers!' cried several guests at once.
Hump-backed Father Christmas then made a complete entry, swinging his huge club, and in a general way clearing the stage for the actors proper –

'Make room, make room, my gallant boys,
And give us space to rhyme;
We've come to show St George's play,
Upon this Christmas time.'

(from *The Return of the Native* by Thomas Hardy)

Superstitions

Superstitions have always been strong among country people. Hardy's famous poem, *The Oxen*, tells of the belief that on Christmas Eve all the animals kneel down in their stalls, just as they were supposed to have done at the birth of Jesus.

Christmas Eve, and twelve of the clock.
'Now they are all on their knees,'
An elder said as we sat in a flock
By the embers in hearthside ease.

We pictured the meek mild creatures where
They dwelt in their stray pen,
Nor did it occur to one of us there
To doubt they were kneeling then.

So fair a fancy few would weave
In these years! Yet, I feel,
If someone said on Christmas Eve,
'Come; see the oxen kneel

In the lonely barton by yonder coomb
Our childhood used to know,'
I should go with him in the gloom,
Hoping it might be so.

Thomas Hardy

? Do you know any superstitions or traditional customs? Many of the old country customs took place on important days, such as May Day, Shrove Tuesday, Good Friday, Easter, Midsummer Eve/Day, Hallowe'en, New Year's Eve/Day, Harvest Time, Twelfth Night.

Find out about as many traditional customs as you can, and what they meant. When and why do you think they began? Do any of them still happen? Are there any particular ones that happen in your area? Have you ever taken part?

Give a short talk about one of the old customs. You may want to illustrate your talk with pictures, objects, songs, rhymes, or actions.

Schools

A ragged school

The Poor Schools

Before the 1870 Education Act most poor children received no schooling. Those that did went to one of a number of little schools. Some were quite good but many were little better than child minders. Parents might have to pay around 1d or 2d a week. The Ragged schools, set up by charities for very poor children and orphans, were free. A Dame school would be run by a woman in her own home, usually for neighbours' children and the standard of education varied greatly. For many children who worked during the week, Sunday schools were their only chance to obtain any basic education. Here they might, if they were lucky, learn to read as well as be taught some elementary religion.

The Education Acts of 1870 and 1880 made it compulsory for all children under ten to go to school. By 1899 the school leaving age was twelve. Elementary schools, also known as Board Schools, were set up. Some of their buildings are still used as schools today. They usually have several brick storeys and separate entrances for Girls and Boys.

(Sherlock Holmes) *'Look at those big, isolated clumps of buildings rising up above the slates, like brick islands in a lead-coloured sea.'*

(Dr Watson) *'The Board Schools.'*

(Holmes) *'Lighthouses, my boy! Beacons of the future! Capsules, with hundreds of bright little seeds in each, out of which will spring the wiser, better England of the future.'*

Can you think of anything today that people might be equally excited about?

The Middle and Upper Classes

In the best families, girls were educated at home by governesses. Some were sent away to the few boarding schools that existed for girls or to a day school. Their curriculum was usually restricted to what was thought to be useful to them in their future domestic lives.

However, the education of boys was thought more important as they would need to be able to earn their living and support their families. Those who could afford it, sent their sons to Public School where they boarded by the term. The less well-off middle classes might send sons to day schools or to board with a country rector who took in a few pupils and charged for their tuition.

GATESHEAD

BRITISH SCHOOL

FOR GIRLS,

In connection with the British School for Boys.

A School on the British or Lancasterian System will be opened for the Education of Girls on

MONDAY, THE 12th OF OCTOBER,

In the spacious SCHOOL ROOM under the

INDEPENDENT CHAPEL, MELBOURNE STREET.

The School will be conducted by MISS WRIGHT, from the British and Foreign School Society, Borough-road, London, of which Society, our gracious Sovereign the QUEEN, is a Patron, and a Subscriber of £100 per Annum; the Lord Bishop of Norwich, and other Dignitaries of the Established Church, are also Patrons and Subscribers.

INHABITANTS OF GATESHEAD,

In this School your Children (above Six Years of Age) will receive a sound Scriptural Education. The Principles on which this School is founded enable it to admit the Children of Parents of every Religious Denomination, while it teaches the Doctrines of Religion from the Page of Divine Inspiration itself, (the introduction of the Sacred Scriptures, without Note or Comment, as the only Book of Religious Instruction, has been from the first a Fundamental Rule in all the Schools of the Society,) it excludes Creeds and Catechisms; and thus, occupying the ground of our Common Christianity, it acts as a Powerful Auxiliary to Sabbath School Instruction, and leaves untouched the Formularies and Discipline of particular Churches.

The great object of the Promoters of these Schools being, that the Children may be Trained to Habits of Industry and Frugality in early life, the Girls will be allowed to bring with them their own Work to Make or Repair.

It is required, that the Girls come to School with their Hands and Faces Clean, their Hair Combed, and their Clothes Whole.

Instructions will be given in Reading, Writing, Arithmetic, Grammar, and Needle-Work.---Mothers will be allowed to send their elder Girls for *half a Day*, if more convenient.

Lectures on various Subjects will be given, during the Winter Evenings, to the Children of both the Schools.

TERMS.---2d. PER WEEK, TO BE PAID IN ADVANCE.

R. H. HAGGIE, Treasurer.

N.B. The British System has been long tried, both in this Country and in the British Colonies, and found to be one of the best Systems of Popular Instruction.

W. DOUGLAS, OBSERVER OFFICE, GATESHEAD.

Discipline and teaching philosophy

The cane was often used in schools of all kinds. Victorians were strong on discipline of children as they believed corporal punishment encouraged respect for the moral life. 'Spare the rod and spoil the child'.

They also placed great importance on teaching facts. Encouraging children to use their imagination was often seen as unnecessary and possibly dangerous. It was thought particularly hazardous for the working classes who might begin to question the way things were run and get ideas above their station! Dickens highlights this closed attitude in his book *Hard Times*, in which Mr Gradgrind says to Mr M'Choakumchild, a new teacher at his school:

> 'Now what I want is, Facts. Teach these boys and girls nothing but Facts. Facts alone are wanted in life. Plant nothing else, and root out everything else. You can only form the minds of reasoning animals upon Facts: nothing else will ever be of any service to them. This is the principle on which I bring up my own children, and this is the principle on which I bring up these children. Stick to Facts, Sir!'

If we only learned facts at school, would we forget how to use our imaginations? Dickens disagreed with Mr Gradgrind and Mr M'Choakumchild. He knew that we all need to dream. Our imaginations can take us anywhere we want and help us to explore ideas.

? Write two paragraphs on the same subject. The first must be entirely made of facts and true statements, like an encyclopaedia entry. In the second, let your imagination wander and describe your thoughts. Choose one of the following subjects: time, the sea, my bedroom, a garden, spaceships, the heart.

Listen to each others' pieces. Which do you find more interesting, and why?

The School Curriculum

Boys who went away to school were taught a wide range of subjects, including English, maths, science, history, geography, philosophy, Latin, Greek and French. Games were considered very important, too, in order to teach boys about fair play and how to work as part of a team. Keeping fit and healthy was also recognised as essential for a healthy mind.

Girls from good families were taught what would fit them for their future lives as wives and mothers in society. Apart from reading and writing, their studies included piano playing, singing, sketching, dancing and curtseying, needlecraft, good manners and deportment, French, and sometimes Italian. On no account were they allowed to play games at school as this was considered unladylike.

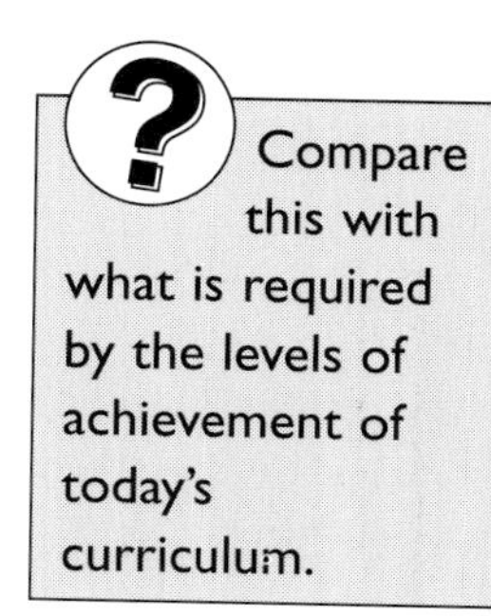

Compare this with what is required by the levels of achievement of today's curriculum.

The New Code of 1879 set out what children should know at each stage of development, very much like the present National Curriculum. The children were tested every year by a visiting Inspector. This table shows what is required in the 'three Rs' – Reading, wRiting and aRithmetic. A 6 year-old should pass at Standard I, while Standard VI was what 11 year-olds should reach.

	Standard I	Standard II	Standard III	Standard IV	Standard V	Standard VI
Reading*	To read a short paragraph from a book, not confined to words of one syllable.	To read with intelligence a short paragraph from an elementary reading book.	To read with intelligence a short paragraph from a more advanced reading book.	To read with intelligence a few lines of prose or poetry selected by the inspector.	Improved reading.	Reading with fluency and expression.
Writing	Copy in manuscript character a line of print, on slates, or in copy books, at choice of managers; and write from dictation a few common words.	A sentence from the same book, slowly read once, and then dictated. Copy books (large or half-text) to be shown.	A sentence slowy dictated once from the same book. Copy books to be shown (small hand, capital letters and figures).	Eight lines slowly dictated once from a reading book. Copy books to be shown (improved small hand).	Writing from memory the substance of a short story read out twice; spelling, grammar, and handwriting to be considered.	A short theme or letter, the composition, spelling, grammar, and handwriting to be considered.
Arithmetic†	Notation and numeration up to 1,000. Simple addition and subtraction of numbers of not more than four figures, and the multiplication tables, to 6 times 12.	Notation and numeration up to 100,000. The four simple rules to short division (inclusive).	Notation and numeration up to 1,000,000. Long division and compound addition and subtraction (money).	Compound rules (money) and reduction (common weights and measures).+	Practice, bills of parcels, and simple proportion.	Proportion, vulgar and decimal fractions.

* 'Reading will be tested in the ordinary class books, if approved by the Inspector, but these books must be of reasonable length and difficulty and unmarked …'

† The work of girls will be judged more leniently than that of boys …'

\+ 'The weights and measures taught in public elementary schools should be only such as are really useful; – such as Avoirdupois Weight, Long Measure, Liquid Measure, Time Table, Square and Cubical Measure, and any measure which is connected with the industrial occupations of the district.'

Reading and Spelling Books

Warne's Victoria Picture Spelling Book was published in 1872 and cost 1 shilling. Often this was the only book used by a child in an elementary school and was used to teach them not only spelling, but also reading, writing, arithmetic, and even history and geography!

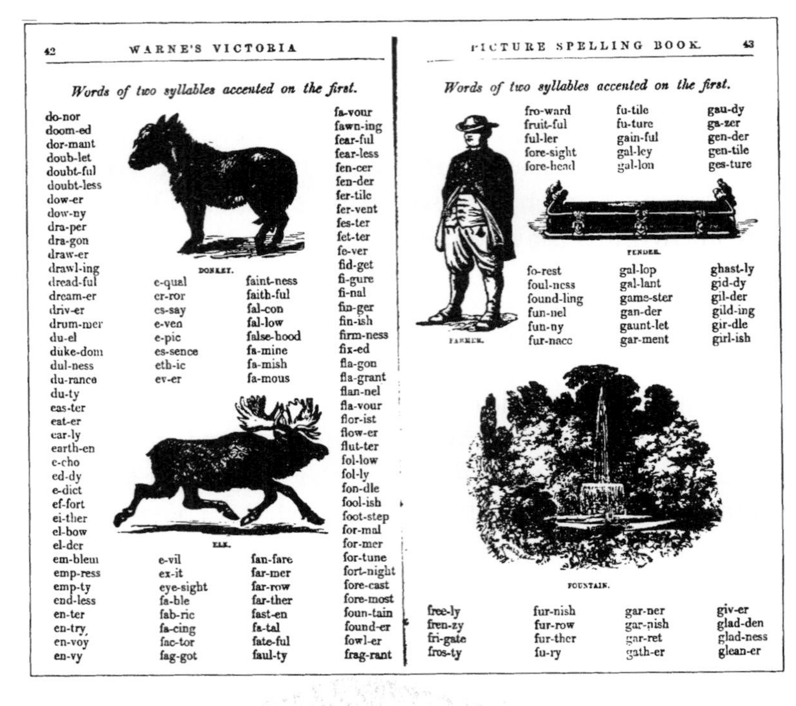

42 WARNE'S VICTORIA

Words of two syllables accented on the first.

do-nor
doom-ed
dor-mant
doub-let
doubt-ful
doubt-less
dow-er
dow-ny
dra-per
dra-gon
draw-er
drawl-ing
dread-ful
dream-er
driv-er
drum-mer
du-el
duke-dom
dul-ness
du-rance
du-ty
eas-ter
eat-er
ear-ly
earth-en
e-cho
ed-dy
e-dict
ef-fort
ei-ther
el-bow
el-der
em-blem
emp-ress
emp-ty
end-less
en-ter
en-try
en-voy
en-vy

DONKEY.

e-qual
er-ror
es-say
e-ven
e-pic
es-sence
eth-ic
ev-er

faint-ness
faith-ful
fal-con
fal-low
false-hood
fa-mine
fa-mish
fa-mous

ELK.

e-vil
ex-it
eye-sight
fa-ble
fab-ric
fa-cing
fac-tor
fag-got

fan-fare
far-mer
far-row
far-ther
fast-en
fa-tal
fate-ful
faul-ty

fa-vour
fawn-ing
fear-ful
fear-less
fen-cer
fen-der
fer-tile
fer-vent
fes-ter
fet-ter
fe-ver
fid-get
fi-gure
fi-nal
fin-ger
fin-ish
firm-ness
fix-ed
fla-gon
fla-grant
flan-nel
fla-vour
flor-ist
flow-er
flut-ter
fol-low
fol-ly
fon-dle
fool-ish
foot-step
for-mal
for-mer
for-tune
fort-night
fore-cast
fore-most
foun-tain
found-er
fowl-er
frag-rant

PICTURE SPELLING BOOK. 43

Words of two syllables accented on the first.

FARMER.

fro-ward
fruit-ful
ful-ler
fore-sight
fore-head

fu-tile
fu-ture
gain-ful
gal-ley
gal-lon

gau-dy
ga-zer
gen-der
gen-tile
ges-ture

FENDER.

fo-rest
foul-ness
found-ling
fun-nel
fun-ny
fur-nace

gal-lop
gal-lant
game-ster
gan-der
gaunt-let
gar-ment

ghast-ly
gid-dy
gil-der
gild-ing
gir-dle
girl-ish

FOUNTAIN.

free-ly
fren-zy
fri-gate
fros-ty

fur-nish
fur-row
fur-ther
fu-ry

gar-ner
gar-nish
gar-ret
gath-er

giv-er
glad-den
glad-ness
glean-er

Reading was often taught by using wall charts. This one is from around 1900. It is based on teaching through phonics and the text uses only words of two or three letters. Although this approach could be helpful, stories were not always very interesting or even sensible! Many children found it difficult to tell the difference between one word and another as they often looked similar in shape and length.

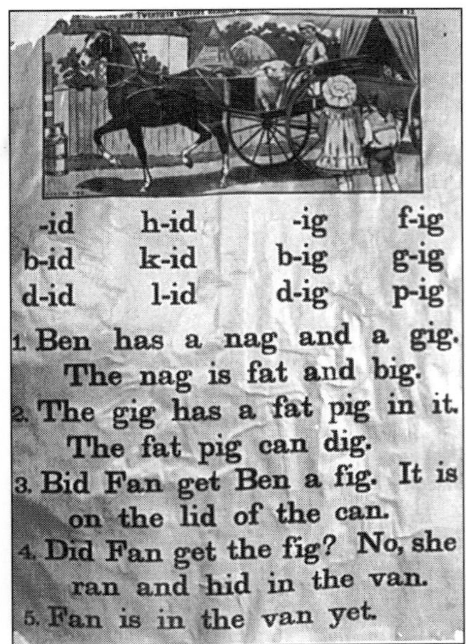

-id h-id -ig f-ig
b-id k-id b-ig g-ig
d-id l-id d-ig p-ig

1. Ben has a nag and a gig. The nag is fat and big.
2. The gig has a fat pig in it. The fat pig can dig.
3. Bid Fan get Ben a fig. It is on the lid of the can.
4. Did Fan get the fig? No, she ran and hid in the van.
5. Fan is in the van yet.

ABC Books

One particular traditional rhyme had been popular for children's books for many years. It was a way of teaching the alphabet and described what different people did to an apple pie. Each letter began a different verb. There are various different versions. This is the beginning of one which was published around 1860. It was called *Darton's Indestructible Apple Pie* – indestructible because it was printed on linen cloth rather than paper.

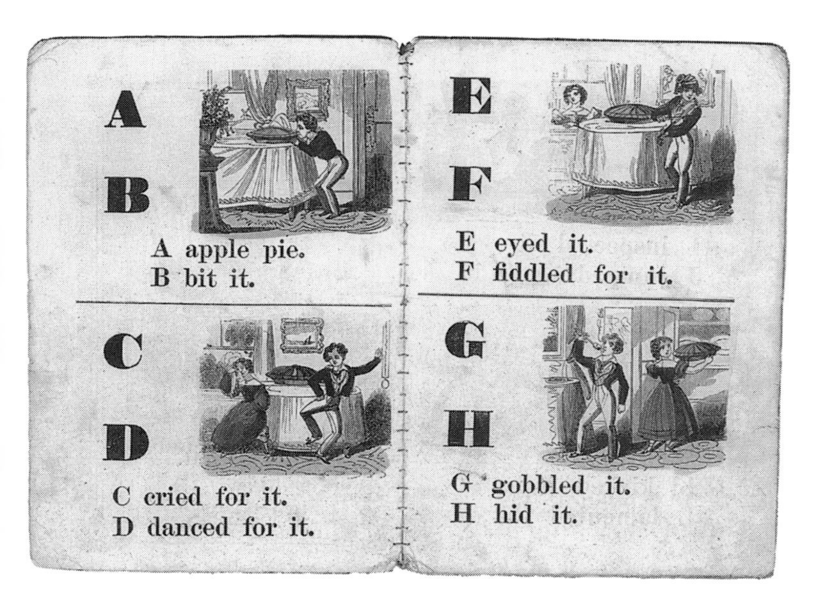
A apple pie.
B bit it.
E eyed it.
F fiddled for it.
C cried for it.
D danced for it.
G gobbled it.
H hid it.

Make an ABC book for a younger child. Start with A was an apple pie and then continue saying what each letter did to it. Each letter of the alphabet thereafter must begin the verb – what was done to the pie – as in the example. Use a dictionary to find interesting and different verbs from the ones in the example. Illustrate each one. You can do this in any way you like, either with drawings, collage, or any other method. Make the book look as professional as you can and, if possible, show and read it to a young child.

Working children

Do ye hear the children weeping, O my brothers,
Ere the sorrow comes with years?
They are leaning their young heads against their mothers, –
And that *cannot stop their tears....*

'For oh,' say the children, 'we are weary,
And we cannot run or leap –
If we cared for any meadows, it were merely
To drop down in them and sleep.
Our knees tremble sorely in the stooping –
We fall upon our faces, trying to go;
And, underneath our heavy eyelids drooping,
The reddest flower would look as pale as snow.
For, all day, we drag our burden tiring,
Through the coal-dark, underground –
Or, all day, we drive the wheels of iron
In the factories, round and round.'

from *The Cry of the Children* by Elizabeth Barrett Browning

The children of the poor had to work in order to survive. They usually began at the age of five or six, working long hours. In the country they were often employed as birdscarers. Elsewhere, others worked in mills, down mines, up chimneys, or scratched a living on the streets. Their lives are described in these extracts by or about real and fictional children.

He lived in the North country, where there were plenty of chimneys to sweep, and plenty of money for Tom to earn and his master to spend. He could neither read nor write, and did not care to do either; and he never washed himself, for there was no water up the court where he lived.... He cried when he had to climb the dark flues, rubbing his poor knees and elbows raw; and when the soot got into his eyes, which it did every day in the week; and when his master beat him, which he did every day in the week; and when he had not enough to eat, which happened every day in the week likewise...

> ...he took all that for the way of the world...and thought of the fine times coming, when he would be a man and a master sweep, and sit in the public-house with a quart of beer and a long pipe, and play cards for silver money, and wear velveteens and ankle-jacks, and keep a white bulldog with one grey ear, and carry her puppies in his pocket, just like a man. And he would have apprentices, one, two, three, if he could. How he would bully them and knock them about, just as his master did to him; and make them carry home the soot sacks, while he rode before them on his donkey, with a pipe in his mouth and a flower in his button-hole, like a king at the head of his army.
>
> Tom, the chimney sweep from *The Water Babies* by Charles Kingsley

Henry Mayhew was a journalist and writer who worked hard to highlight and change the terrible conditions suffered by poor people. He interviewed many of the poorest people and published his surveys in several books; here is an extract from an interview he had with a boy who made a living scavenging in the sewers of London:

> **?** Discuss this extract with a friend. Do you find anything in it particularly striking? What do you think Charles Kingsley wants the reader to feel about Tom?

> I'd put down my arm to my shoulder in the mud and bring up shillings and half-crowns, and lots of coppers, and plenty of other things. I once found a silver jug as big as a quart pot,... There's some places,... where they say there's foul air, and they tells me the foul air 'ill cause instantious death, but I niver met with anythink about it,... I've often seed as many as a hundred rats at once, and they're whoppers in the sewers,... a cove can't stop in longer than six or seven hours, 'cause of the tide, you must be out before that's up.

This is from William Dyson's evidence to the Commission on Children's Employment, set up by parliament in 1842 to investigate conditions of work.

> 'I am a hurrier. [someone who hauled the full coal trucks from the coalface] I am fourteen years old and have been employed ever since I was six. I come to work at seven o'clock, and sometimes leave at four, five or six in the evening in summer, and in the winter near seven. I live half a mile from the pit and take my dinner with me, which is a dry muffin. I have not time to get my dinner in the pit, but eat it on my way home. I have nothing to drink. When I get home I sometimes get potatoes and meat. Our workings from the shaft are 500 yards and I have to hurry the corves [coal trucks] full that distance and bring them back empty...
>
> [continued overleaf]

Choose one of the following activities:

Imagine you are a Victorian social reformer. Using information from the extracts on these pages, write a newspaper or magazine article telling your readers why something must be done to help children.

Look back at Elizabeth Barrett Browning's poem at the beginning of this section. Write your own poem about the plight of a working child. You do not have to write about a Victorian child – you could think about children today who are forced to work at a very young age.

[continued from previous page]

… We have but one girl working with us, by name Ann Ambler. She gets 6/- a week. She hurries by herself and has to hurry the same weight and distance as I have; there is not a bit of difference between any of us. I have seen her thrashed many times when she does not please the hewers [miners]; they rap her in the face and knock her down. She does not like the work, she does not that. I have seen her cry many times.'

The following extract comes from Elizabeth Gaskell's novel, *North and South*. Bessy Higgins tells Margaret Hale how she came to be so ill after working in a cotton mill.

'– and the fluff got into my lungs, and poisoned me… there's many a one as works in a carding-room, that falls into a waste, coughing and spitting blood, because they're just poisoned by the fluff… Some folk have a great wheel at one end o' their carding-rooms to make a draught, and carry off th' dust; but that wheel costs a deal o' money… and brings in no profit; so it's but a few of the masters as will put 'em up…'

Crossing sweepers

Victorian town and city streets were dirty, with mud and horse droppings from the horse-drawn cabs, buses and carts. Some managed made a small living by sweeping paths over roads for people to cross or by collecting manure. Here are some of the things they told Henry Mayhew about their lives:

'I don't like the sweeping, and I don't think there's e'er a one of us wot likes it. In the winter we has to be out in the cold, and then in summer we have to sleep out all night… we go eight or ten of us into a doorway of the church,… The most of the boys has got no homes.'

'I'm twelve years old,… Since mother's been dead, I've had to mind my little brother and sister, so that I haven't been to school; but when I goes a crossing-sweeping I takes them along with me… Sister's three and a-half year old, and brother's five year, so he's just beginning to help me.'

Public health

Rats!

They fought the dogs and killed the cats,
And bit the babies in the cradles,
And ate the cheeses out of the vats,
And licked the soup from the cooks' own ladles,
Split open the kegs of salted sprats,
Made nests inside men's Sunday hats,
And even spoiled the women's chats
By drowning their speaking
With shrieking and squeaking
In fifty different sharps and flats.

(from *The Pied Piper of Hamelin* by Robert Browning)

A DROP OF LONDON WATER.

Browning's picture of the rats in Hamelin could be seen any day in the poorer areas of any large Victorian town or city. Everywhere there were sewer rats, filthy and smelly, who helped to spread horrible diseases. Rats really did gnaw at the faces and fingers of babies and young children who lived in the slums and crowded lodging houses. It was no wonder that in 1848 and 1853 cholera swept through London and elsewhere like the plague; and in 1858 the pollution of the River Thames smelt so bad, particularly the mud at low tide, that people crossing bridges were often sick and Members of Parliament were forced to leave their work and escape from Westminster. People called this The Year of the Great Stink!

CHOLERA
AND
WATER.

BOARD OF WORKS
FOR THE LIMEHOUSE DISTRICT,
Comprising Limehouse, Ratcliff, Shadwell, and Wapping.

The INHABITANTS of the District within which CHOLERA IS PREVAILING, are earnestly advised

NOT TO DRINK ANY WATER
WHICH HAS NOT
PREVIOUSLY BEEN BOILED.

Fresh Water ought to be Boiled every Morning for the day's use, and what remains of it ought to be thrown away at night. The Water ought not to stand where any kind of dirt can get into it, and great care ought to be given to see that Water Butts and Cisterns are free from dirt.

BY ORDER,

THOS. W. RATCLIFF,
CLERK OF THE BOARD.

[illegible]

From surveys at the time, we can see how bad things were all over the country. Here the Town Clerk of Macclesfield describes what some of his officials found when they visited some lodging premises (a privy is a toilet):

> In four small cottages there was an average of 188 persons lodged; they had a small yard, and the remains only of what had been two privies, all the ordure being in the open yard ... In another lodging house there were three small rooms upstairs: in the first were 16 men, women and children, lying together on the floor; in the second there were twelve, also on the floor; and a third room was used as a privy, the boarded floor being literally covered with human ordure ... In another lodging-house there was a bed on which lay a woman in the pains of labour; by her side lay a man apparently asleep, and ten other men, women and children were in the same room ...

In this extract from Elizabeth Gaskell's novel, *Mary Barton*, we are given a vivid picture of life for the poor in Manchester:

> (The street) ... was unpaved; and down the middle a gutter forced its way, every now and then forming pools in the holes with which the street abounded ... women from their doors tossed household slops of every description into the gutter; they ran into the next pool, which overflowed and stagnated; ... You went down one step even from the foul area into the cellar in which a family of human beings lived. It was very dark inside. The window-panes were many of them broken and stuffed with rags...
>
> ... on going into the cellar ... the smell was so foetid as almost to knock the two men down ... they began to ... see three or four little children rolling on the damp, nay wet, brick floor, through which the stagnant, filthy moisture of the street oozed up; the fire-place was empty and black; the wife sat on her husband's chair, and cried in the dank loneliness.

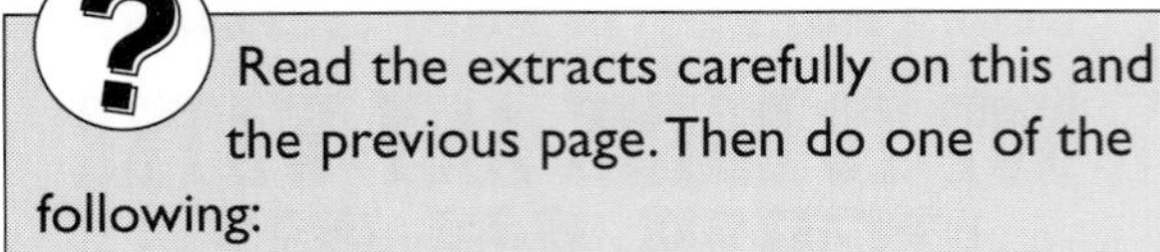

Read the extracts carefully on this and the previous page. Then do one of the following:

Imagine you are living in London in the Year of the Great Stink. Write a letter to your MP complaining about the terrible conditions and asking him to take some action.

You have just moved into a slum area of a city. Write to an old friend in the country, describing the type of conditions that you live in.

CLEAN WATER

In 1848, the City of London's first Medical Officer of Health, Sir John Simon, began the task of laying down a drainage system in the capital. This meant that sewage could be washed through pipes away from houses and emptied much further down the river where it would be swept out to sea. By 1865 London's drainage was complete, and other cities and towns were well under way with their systems.

Vermin

Everyone suffered from rats and other types of vermin such as beetles, mice, fleas and lice. Here is a 'household hint' for the housewife from a book of the time.

RATS CAN BE DRIVEN OUT OF A HOUSE by depriving them of water. They can live almost indefinitely without food, and, when hard pushed, will not hesitate to eat each other, but no rat can go twenty-four hours without drink, and if every possible means of obtaining water is taken from them, they will desert the vicinity.

Alfred Domett entered the following in his diary for 3 June 1875: all about Admiral Hall's 'old waddling terrier'.

He says their kitchen is terribly infested with black beetles, and the dog always sleeps there at night and has become so fond of them that if anyone, even himself, goes in after the servants are gone to bed, and attempts to kill any of them, the dog will try to bite him, and do all he can to prevent their being molested by barking and showing his anger. No doubt the dog lying awake, or in a dog-sleep, so much alone, has come to like the companionship even of the beetles, perhaps feels their rushing about even an amusement.

No. D 171.
THE "DEMON" BEETLE TRAPS.
Bait with White Sugar.
Succeeds where others fail.
In constant use in large Bakeries, Coffee Palaces, Confectioners Shops, Government Departments, Hospitals, Hotels, Public Institutions, Restaurants, and on the Liners of the leading Steamship Companies.
The most successful Trap yet introduced.
Each 1/3
For other descriptions, see Guide, pages 434 & 974.

Rat-pits

A popular sport was rat-killing by dogs. Ratting meetings were held at 'Ratpits' in public houses and people bet on the number of rats a dog would kill in a set time. Notices for 'Rats Wanted' and 'Rats Bought and Sold' would go up and some ratting houses were said to take in between three and seven hundred rats every week. Best-quality rats, such as barn rats from the country, fetched up to a shilling each; smelly sewer rats, who often infected the dogs' mouths, could usually be had for half-a-crown a dozen. A dog was put into a large pit with a number of rats and killed as many as it could while spectators watched and cheered.

? Choose one of the following:

Design a 'RATS WANTED' poster for a ratpit in 1850.

Write a short story about an encounter with rats, mice or cockroaches. You can set your story in Victorian times or the present.

Police and detection

The first police force, the Metropolitan Police, was set up in London in 1829 by Sir Robert Peel who was then Home Secretary. There were 1,000 of these blue-coated policemen who became known as 'Peelers' or 'Bobbies' (after Robert Peel). By 1856 there were police forces in most parts of the country.

By the end of the century, reading about crime was very popular, particularly with the working classes who enjoyed newspapers, such as *The Illustrated Police News*. These sensational publications told of criminal cases, often in picture stories, and were bought at weekends when people had time to read them.

Jack the Ripper

One of the most famous cases of Victorian times concerned the violent murders of five prostitutes in Whitechapel in the East End of London. They all took place between 1 August and 9 November 1888, and the murderer was never caught. He was known first as 'Leather Apron', and later, as details of his gruesome methods of mutilating the bodies became known, the newspapers began to call him 'Jack the Ripper'.

The Metropolitan Police suspected a number of people at the time, many of them highly unlikely. It was suggested that the murderer might have been a doctor because of the way he had carved the bodies. This theory captured popular imagination after the successful dramatisation of Robert Louis Stevenson's *Dr Jekyll and Mr Hyde*, which was showing in a London theatre at the same time. The leading actor was so convincing as he changed from the decent Dr Jekyll into the bestial Mr Hyde that even he was suspected for a while.

When the murders suddenly stopped the police believed that the man had either died, been sent to a lunatic asylum, or had left the country. (Their main suspect actually committed suicide.) Even now, over a century later, theories are still being suggested as to who Jack the Ripper was.

Methods of detection

In those early days detection was difficult. There was no advanced forensic work, no DNA sampling, and no finger-printing. Solving a crime depended on finding clues around the scene of the crime, eye-witness accounts, or the culprit being caught in the act; or sometimes on a policeman having a 'hunch'. Police detectives were often shown as none too bright in the popular detective stories. Sergeant Cuff, in *The Moonstone* by Wilkie Collins, makes some very basic mistakes, and Inspector Lestrade, in the Sherlock Holmes stories, is generally shown as honest but plodding.

There was a popular belief that the last thing a dying person sees becomes imprinted on their eyes. One of the police lines of enquiry into the Ripper murders was to photograph the eyes of one of the Ripper's victims in the hope that they would find a picture of her attacker. Even Queen Victoria, who took a close interest in the Ripper case, was moved to write to her Prime Minister, the Marquis of Salisbury:

> *'This new ghastly murder shows the absolute necessity for some very decided action . . . our detectives (must be) improved. They are not what they should be.'*

Cartoon from Punch, *mocking police attempts at catching the Ripper.*

Detection did eventually improve, but it was a fictional detective, Sherlock Holmes, who was mainly responsible for changes in detective work.

Look back at the page from *The Illustrated London Police News*. Either on your own or in pairs, choose one of the *Sherlock Holmes* short stories to illustrate for the newspaper. Read the story, and then draw the main events, showing the crime and how it is solved by Holmes and Watson.

Try to present your sketches and text in the same style as in *The Illustrated London Police News*.

The Great Detective – Sherlock Holmes

In the following passage, Sherlock Holmes explains to Dr Watson how the science of deduction works:

> *Observation with me is second nature … I knew you came from Afghanistan …The train of reasoning ran: 'Here is a gentleman of a medical type, but with the air of a military man. Clearly an army doctor then. He has just come from the tropics, for his face is dark, and that is not the natural tint of his skin, for his wrists are fair. He has undergone hardship and sickness, as his haggard face says clearly. His left arm has been injured. He holds it in a stiff and unnatural manner. Where in the tropics could an English army doctor have seen much hardship and got his arm wounded? Clearly in Afghanistan.' The whole train of thought did not occupy a second. I then remarked that you came from Afghanistan, and you were astonished.*
>
> (from *A Study in Scarlet*, Part 1, Chap 2)

Sir Arthur Conan Doyle

Sherlock Holmes was invented by the writer Sir Arthur Conan Doyle, and he made his first appearance in the story *A Study in Scarlet*, in 1887. Sir Arthur Conan Doyle was able to use the knowledge he had gained as a doctor in his books. Sherlock Holmes' methods influenced the way police worked all over the world. He introduced ideas such as the use of Plaster of Paris to take casts of footprints, the examination of dust in clothes to help place someone at the scene of the crime, and the analysis of different tobacco ash in order to identify brands of cigar. Police forces in both China and Egypt used the stories as part of their official police training and the American FBI also studied his methods.

? Every year, thousands of people write to Sherlock Holmes. Discuss with your friends any questions you would like to ask him. One of you write a letter to him – you will receive a reply from his secretary. Enclose a stamped addressed envelope for the reply. Address it to:

Sherlock Holmes, Esq.
221B Baker Street,
London NW1

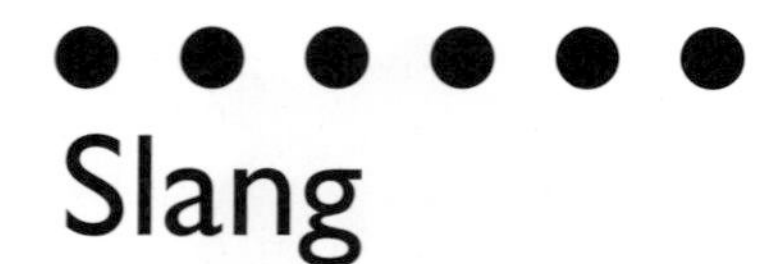

Slang

Slang is a special jargon, or vocabulary, used by certain groups of people. It is usually used in speech rather than in formal writing, although diaries, letters and newspaper articles often include slang. The words and phrases tend to be more colourful and expressive than ordinary Standard English; for example, instead of saying 'Go away!', you might hear 'Hop it!' or 'Make yourself scarce!'. Slang changes and goes out of fashion very quickly. You can often tell how old someone is by the slang they use.

Read Mr Pooter's diary entries concerning his son Lupin's use of slang:

November 16: ... Lupin appeared, with a yellow complexion, and said: 'Hulloh! Guv., what priced head have you this morning?' I told him he might just as well speak to me in Dutch. He added: 'When I woke this morning, my head was as big as Baldwin's balloon.'...

November 18: ... we declined the invitation ... to Miss Bird's wedding. Lupin said: 'I am with you for once. To my mind a wedding's a very poor play. There are only two parts in it – the bride and bridegroom. The best man is only a walking gentleman. With the exception of a crying father and a snivelling mother, the rest are supers who have to dress well and have to pay for their insignificant parts in the shape of costly presents.' I did not care for the theatrical slang, but thought it clever, though disrespectful.

May 13: ...[Lupin] said: 'I met an old friend ... He's a jolly, good, all-round sort of fellow, and a very different stamp from that inflated fool of a Perkupp [Mr Pooter's boss] ... I have done no injury. Crowbillon is simply tired of a stagnant stick-in-the-mud firm, and made the change on his own account. I simply recommended the new firm as a matter of biz – good old biz!' I said quietly: 'I don't understand your slang, and at my time of life have no desire to learn it'...

from *The Diary of a Nobody,* by George & Weedon Grossmith

Every job, profession and class has its own slang, but perhaps the largest group always inventing new slang is young people. Parents, like Mr Pooter, often despair of their children's slang expressions, and by the time they have worked out what things mean the words are already out of date!

? What slang expressions do you use? Discuss them as a class, and make a list of them. Do the adults in your life understand them? Do you want them to?

Victorian slang words

Words for 'very good'

fizzing tremendous galoptious ripping splendacious scrumdolious uncommon bang-up capital spiffing swell tip-top stunning splendiferous

? Make a list of as many 20th century slang expressions which you already know, or can find out, meaning 'very good'. Does anybody still use any of the Victorian ones today?

'A merry Christmas, uncle! God save you!' cried a cheerful voice. It was the voice of Scrooge's nephew, who came upon him so quickly that this was the first intimation he had of his approach.

'Bah!' said Scrooge, 'Humbug!' … 'Merry Christmas! Out upon Merry Christmas!'

from *A Christmas Carol* by Charles Dickens

Words for 'nonsense'

Bosh! Humbug! Footle! Skittles! Barnet! Bladderdash! Flapdoodle! Blather! Gammon and Spinach! Kibosh! Poppycock! Bunkum! Gammon! Tosh! Barrikin! Fandangle!

? How many slang expressions meaning 'nonsense' do you know or can you find? What words do you say? Ask people of different ages and generations what their expressions for this are. Are there differences?

(Some words you collect may be quite coarse, eg 'crap!', but this is often the nature of slang. Dictionaries of slang do not avoid including them, so neither need you.)

Words for parts of the body

head – top-piece, nut
hair – nob-thatch
face – glass case
eyes – peepers, lamps, top lights, front windows, blinkers
nostrils – snufflers
mouth – rattletrap
teeth – rattlers
hands – grabbers, grapplers
feet – trotters, walkers, steppers

Slang from the Empire

Soldiers brought new slang into the English language when they picked up words from places in the British Empire. The following expressions come from India:

Chokey = a prison (from chauki, a four-sided building)

Doolally = mad (from Deolali, a town near Bombay, which had a mental hospital for British troops)

Have a shufti = have a look

Khyber Pass = a rhyming slang word for a part of the body (from the place name)

Kennings

Several Victorian slang expressions took the form of Kennings. Originally occurring in Anglo-Saxon, a Kenning is a new descriptive name for something. It is usually in two parts, separated by a hyphen, and tells us what the thing is like or what it does.

The following are Victorian slang kennings for different kinds of people:

catgut-scraper (violinist) domino-thumper (pianist) sheepskin-fiddler (drummer)
cackle-chucker (stage prompter) curtain-taker (actor) rhyme-slinger (poet)
devil-dodger (clergyman) carrion-hunter (undertaker) beach-tramper (coastguard)
sole-slogger (shoemaker) vowel-mauler (indistinct speaker) boot-licker (a creep)

? Make up some Kennings for modern people's jobs or occupations, for example, wave-rider (surfer), dough-basher (baker) or fever-soother (nurse).

Underworld slang

Charles Dickens' character, Fagin, in the novel *Oliver Twist*, was what was known as a 'kidsman'. He trained children, often runaways from the workhouse, to steal for him, in return for food and shelter. This life could be better and kinder than they had known before. This extract describes Fagin's boys, Dodger and Bates, showing new recruit Oliver how to become a tailer, smatter-hauler and dipper (a pickpocket).

> At last the Dodger trod under his [Fagin's] toes, or ran upon his boot accidentally, while Charley Bates stumbled up against him behind: and in that one moment they took from him with extraordinary rapidity, snuff box, note-case, watch-guard, chain, shirt-pin, pocket handkerchief, even the spectacle case. If the old gentleman felt a hand in one of his pockets, he cried out where it was; and then the game began all over again.

Petty thieves were generally known as gonophs, but each speciality had its own name; eg palmer = shoplifter, flimp = a snatch pickpocket, maltooler = pickpocket on buses, mutcher = stealer from drunks. Naturally, they also had their own words for the police, such as bluebottles, frogs, crushers, miltonians, pigs and jacks. (Do you know any modern slang words for the police or thieves?) Many also had what seemed to be completely different languages which they used to stop others listening in to their conversations.

Rhyming slang

One of the best known of these is Cockney Rhyming Slang which was invented in the Victorian era. Instead of saying the name of something, you use a pair of words which rhyme with it. For example, bees and honey (money), elephant's trunk (drunk), and linen-draper (paper, therefore news). Very often the second, rhyming part, was dropped. This made it even more difficult for outsiders to understand. Some of these survive today in everyday speech, such as 'to rabbit' from rabbit and pork (talk), 'take a butcher's' from butcher's hook (a look) 'a grass' (informer) from grasshopper (copper/policeman).

Can you work out what the following rhyming slang expressions mean?

Parts of the body: Hampstead Heath (Hampsteads), Barnet Fair, North and South, Plates of meat, Glass-case, Mince Pies.

Clothing: Daisy Roots (Daisies), Turtle Doves (Turtles), Whistle and Flute (Whistle), Tit for tat (Titfer), Dicky Dirt (Dicky).

Types of people: Trouble and Strife, Holy Friar and Tea Leaf (not to be trusted).

Make up some new rhyming slang of your own. Your new expressions can be for anything you choose, such as clothing, food, activities or places.

Write a short dramatic scene between two people having a discussion about anything you like. (The subject certainly does not have to be about criminal activity!) Use as many of your new rhyming slang expressions as possible.

Act out your scene to others. Are they able to follow what is going on? Or does the rhyming slang make it difficult? How effective against eavesdroppers do you think rhyming slang would have been for Victorian criminals?

Backslang

Another kind of secret language was invented in the 19th century by traders and street sellers. This was called 'backslang' and worked by pronouncing some words backwards. For example, a delo diam was an old maid, a dab tros was a bad sort, and an efink was a knife. At least one of these backslang words is still used by many people today – yob. They, too, had their own word for a policeman – esclop (pronounced 'slop'). Sometimes they added or changed the places of letters to make the words easier to say, or perhaps to disguise them more.

For example, enin yanneps (nine pennies), delog (gold) and evatch (have).

Can you work out what the following backslang words mean?

enob rats erif emit epip neergs taf nammow
rouf sretsio edgabac sreswort I evatch eno esuch and eno esroch

Count to ten in Victorian backslang

eno owt erth rouf evif xis neves teaich enin net

Make up some of your own backslang words and try to hold a conversation using them with a friend.

Popular wordgames

Acrostics

An Acrostic is a poem, or a puzzle, where a word, phrase or name is spelt out by the first letters of each line. During the Victorian period, acrostics became something of a craze. Several books completely full of acrostics were published and Acrostic Clubs sprang up. Making and solving acrostics was a popular entertainment at dinner parties among the middle and upper classes.

This one is an ode to Prince Albert and the Crystal Palace:

A*ccomplish'd Prince! from whose aesthetic mind,*
L*ike Hamlet's, philosophic and refin'd,*
B*urst the bright vision of that Palace fair,*
E*nchanting wondering nations gather'd there:*
R*are favourite of fortune! well, I ween,* (ween = think, believe)
T*hou art fit consort, worthy of our Queen.*

Queen Victoria was said to be particularly keen on the double acrostic, where words can be read from both the first and last letters. It is thought that she actually made up the following acrostic puzzle for her children. The first letters spell the name of an English town. The last letters, read upwards, tell what it is famous for:

CLUES	ANSWERS
A city in Italy	(**N**aple**S**)
A river in Germany	(**E**lb**E**)
A town in the United States	(**W**ashingto**N**)
A town in North America	(**C**incinnat**I**)
A town in Holland	(**A**msterda**M**)
The Turkish name of Constantinople	(**S**tambou**L**)
A town in Bothnia	(**T**orne**A**)
A city in Greece	(**L**epant**O**)
A circle on the globe	(**E**clipti**C**)

Make up your own Acrostic poem or puzzle. Either:

write an acrostic ode about a famous Victorian person using information you have discovered from your reading. Each line must begin with the next letter of the person's name, and the whole poem must make sense and be written in a natural way. It should not just be a list of phrases. And it will have to rhyme! Or:

make up an Acrostic puzzle, like Queen Victoria's. You will need to write a series of clues for each word of the final acrostic. It may be a single or double acrostic. (Dictionaries will help you find words beginning and ending with the letters you need.) For example:

The whole means when schoolchildren take a break

The opposite of war (5 letters)	(**P**eac**E**)
Roman name for England's capital city (9)	(**L**ondiniu**M**)
Proof of being somewhere else when a crime has occurred (5)	(**A**lib**I**)
A type of sailing boat (5)	(**Y**ach**T**)

Word Squares

Another favourite pastime was making up word squares. These are created from words of equal length which read the same across and down.

Some Victorian examples:

C	R	E	W
R	A	V	E
E	V	E	R
W	E	R	E

C	R	E	S	T
R	E	A	C	H
E	A	G	E	R
S	C	E	N	E
T	H	R	E	E

M	I	G	H	T
I	D	L	E	R
G	L	I	D	E
H	E	D	G	E
T	R	E	E	S

Make up a word square puzzle. You need to find the words first and then write clues for them. Swap clues with a friend and see if you can solve each other's puzzles. For example:

CLUES

Fighting between enemies (3 letters)	(W A R)
The first playing card in the pack	(A C E)
The colour of warning or danger	(R E D)

Univocalics

(The Approach of Evening)

Idling, I sit in this mild twilight dim,
Whilst birds, in wild, swift vigils, circling skim.
Light winds in sighing sink, till, rising bright,
Night's Virgin Pilgrim swims in vivid light!

Gleanings for the Curious (1890) by C C Bombaugh

Univocalics are pieces of writing (poems or prose) which use only one of the five vowels (a, e, i, o or u). Which vowel does the above example use?

A famous univocalic rhyming couplet about keeping the ten commandments is said to have been carved on an altar. It appeared in W T Dobson's *Literary Frivolities* (1880). It is often printed without any vowels.

Can you solve it? Use your chosen vowel as many times as you like.

P R S V R Y P R F C T M N

V R K P T H S P R C P T S T N

Try writing your own univocalic piece. First, collect as many words as you can which use only one vowel. Dictionaries will help with this. Then start with a simple sentence. Make sure that what you say makes sense. For example:

Old dogs do not go on for long.

Fat cats can't catch rats.

Then see if you can write a longer piece – either a rhyming poem or a short story.

Poets

Alfred, Lord Tennyson (1809–92)

I went down to see Tennyson, who is very peculiar-looking, tall, dark, with a fine head, long black flowing hair, and a beard; oddly dressed, but there is no affectation about him. I told him how much I admired his glorious lines to my precious Albert, and how much comfort I found in his In Memoriam. He was full of unbounded appreciation of beloved Albert. When he spoke of my loss, of that to the nation, his eyes quite filled with tears.

(from Queen Victoria's diary; 14 April 1862)

Tennyson was the best-known Victorian poet. He began his long poem, *In Memoriam,* out of grief after the death of his good friend, Arthur Hallam, in 1833. It was finally published in 1850, the year he was made poet to the royal household (Poet Laureate), a post he held for 42 years.

? Read Tennyson's poem aloud. Notice how it rhymes, and listen to the 4-beat rhythm of each line. Did you also hear any alliteration (neighbouring words beginning with the same sound)?

Write your own poem aloud about a wild creature, using the same rhyme and rhythm pattern as Tennyson. Try to use some alliteration, too, eg: *The Mole* – He shoves up soil with shoulders strong…

The Eagle

He clasps the crag with crooked hands;
Close to the sun in lonely lands,
Ring'd with the azure world, he stands.

The wrinkled sea beneath him crawls;
He watches from his mountain walls,
And like a thunderbolt he falls.

The Brownings

Oh, to be in England,
Now that April's there,
And whoever wakes in England
Sees, some morning, unaware,
That the lowest boughs and the brushwood sheaf
Round the elm-tree bole are in tiny leaf,
While the chaffinch sings on the orchard bough
In England – now!

from *Home-Thoughts From Abroad* by Robert Browning (1812–89)

Robert Browning and his wife, Elizabeth Barrett Browning, were forced to live abroad. They had met and fallen in love after writing to each other. However, Elizabeth's father had forbidden any of his children to marry, so in 1846 the two eloped to Italy. Elizabeth had very modern ideas and was interested in politics, and during her lifetime was considered a better poet than Robert (see poem on page 34).

Elizabeth Barrett Browning

Elizabeth was a semi-invalid all her adult life, due to hurting her spine in an accident. She died after 15 years of married life. Robert returned to live with his sister in England. He also had many writers and artists as friends. One of Robert's last poems was in response to reading a letter of the writer, Edward Fitzgerald, which had been published after his death. The letter said:

> 'Mrs Browning's death is rather a relief to me, I must say – A woman of real genius, I know, but what is the upshot of it all! She and her sex had better mind the kitchen and her children, and perhaps the poor. Except in such things as little novels, they only devote themselves to what men do much better, leaving that which men do worse or not at all.'

Although it was 28 years since his wife's death, Browning was so angry and upset that he wrote the following poem:

I chanced upon a new book yesterday;
I opened it; and where my finger lay,
'Twixt page and uncut page, these words I read
– Some six or seven, at most – and learned thereby
That you, Fitzgerald, whom by ear and eye
She never knew, 'thanked God my wife was dead'.

Ay dead, and were yourself alive, good Fitz,
How to return your thanks would task my wits.
Kicking you seems the common lot of curs –
While more appropriate greeting lends you grace:
Surely, to spit there glorifies your face –
Spitting – from lips once sanctified by Hers.

Christina Rossetti (1830–94)

What Are Heavy?

What are heavy? Sea-sand and sorrow;
What are brief? Today and tomorrow;
What are frail? Spring blossoms and youth;
What are deep? The ocean and truth.

? Write a poem using the same pattern as Christina Rossetti. You might try some of the following, or make up your own questions to answer. What are light? What are old? What are shallow? What are cold?

Christina Rossetti

Dante Gabriel and Christina were brother and sister. He was a successful painter who was a founder member of a group of artists, poets and critics who called themselves the Pre-Raphaelite Brotherhood. Although he was also successful as a poet, it is Christina's work which has lasted. She suffered ill health most of her life and her poems often show a sadness and a looking forward to death. She described herself as 'grown old before my time'.

Thomas Hardy (1840–1928)

Thomas Hardy made his name writing novels but his last two books, *Tess of the D'Urbervilles* (1891) and *Jude the Obscure* (1895), were not liked by many. So Hardy began to publish his poetry instead. He believed in writing in language close to speech and not in the very flowery fashion of most Victorian poets. He was a master of rhythm, rhyme and form. However, it was not until later in the 20th century that people began to appreciate his poetry (see poem on page 27).

Gerard Manley Hopkins (1844–89)

Gerard Manley Hopkins was a Jesuit priest. He published nothing during his lifetime, mainly because the few poems he sent to editors were rejected. They did not like his new kind of writing with its sprung rhythm, internal rhyme and alliteration. After his death from typhoid, his poems went to his great friend, the poet Robert Bridges, who eventually published them in 1918.

***from* Spring**

Nothing is so beautiful as Spring –
When weeds, in wheels, shoot long and lovely and lush;
Thrush's eggs look little low heavens, and thrush
Through the echoing timber does so rinse and wring
The ear, it strikes like lightnings to hear him sing;
The glassy peartree leaves and blooms, they brush
The descending blue; that blue is all in a rush
With richness; the racing lambs too have fair their fling.

Gerard Manley Hopkins

Lewis Carroll (1832–98) and his wordgames

'He is moreover marvellously ingenious in replacing the ordinary inflexions of nouns and verbs, as detailed in our grammars, by more exact analogies, or convenient forms of his own devising. This source of fault will in due time exhaust itself though flowing freely at present ... You may fairly anticipate for him a bright career.'

(from Charles Lutwidge Dodgson's school report in 1844)

Little did his teachers realise that this 12 year old's love of language play would make him famous. Charles Lutwidge Dodgson was the real name of Lewis Carroll. (He used versions of his first two names for his pseudonym – Lewis/Lutwidge and Carroll/Charles.) He was a gifted mathematician who lectured at Oxford University and wrote books under his real name, as well as being a good photographer. However, it is as the author of the 'Alice' books and nonsense verse that he became famous.

Alice's Adventures in Wonderland and *Through the Looking-Glass* were made up for Alice Liddell, the young daughter of the Dean of his Oxford college. They take place in topsy-turvy worlds where nothing is quite what it seems. Look at the first verse of *Jabberwocky* from *Through the Looking-Glass* and Humpty Dumpty's explanation of the few words:

Jabberwocky

'Twas brillig, and the slithy toves
Did gyre and gimble in the wabe
All mimsy were the borogoves,
And the mome raths outgrabe.

An illustration for 'Jabberwocky' *by Sir John Tenniel, one of the finest illustrators and cartoonists of the era.*

'That's enough to begin with,' Humpty Dumpty interrupted: 'there are plenty of hard words there. 'Brillig' means four o'clock in the afternoon – the time when you begin broiling things for dinner.'
'That'll do very well,' said Alice: 'and slithy?'
'Well, 'slithy' means 'lithe and slimy.' 'Lithe' is the same as 'active.' You see it's a portmanteau – there are two meanings packed into one word.'
'I see it now,' Alice remarked thoughtfully: 'and what are 'toves'?' …
'Well, 'toves' are something like badgers – they're something like lizards – and they're something like corkscrews.'
'They must be very curious-looking creatures.'
'They are that,' said Humpty Dumpty: 'also they make their nests under sundials – also they live on cheese.'

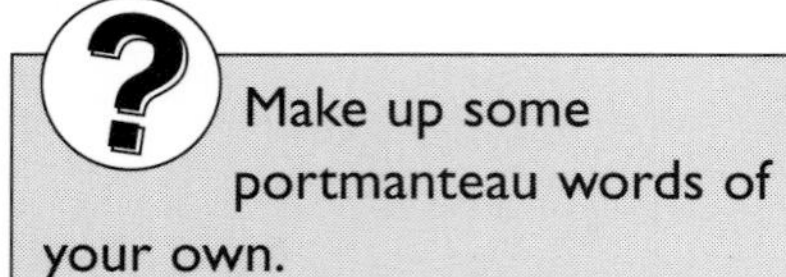

Make up some portmanteau words of your own.

Find a copy of the whole of *Jabberwocky* and write down or underline all the made up words in the poem. How do you think Humpty Dumpty might explain them? Write down your definitions.

NEW WORDS

Of the words that Carroll coined (invented) in the poem, three have even entered the English language and are now in the dictionary – chortle, burble and galumph. Some are examples of what he called portmanteau words. These are words made from the sense and sound of two (or more) other words. For example:
slimy + lithe = slithy
flimsy + miserable = mimsy
bleat + murmur + warble = burble

FAMOUS QUOTATIONS FROM THE *ALICE* BOOKS

Off with her head!

Jam to-morrow and jam yesterday – but never jam to-day.

But answer came there none.

As large as life, and twice as natural.

It's my own invention.

Curiouser and curiouser!

The time has come, the Walrus said, To talk of many things–

Lewis Carroll also invented the idea of the 'Un-birthday present', reasoning that you have only 1 birthday, but 364 un-birthdays!

Lewis Carroll's wordgames

Anagrams

Carroll loved anagrams, which are words or phrases made from all the letters of other words. They are often a description of a person made from the letters of their name.

Two of his anagrams were on Victorian politicians:

DISRAELI = I LEAD, SIR!

WILLIAM EWART GLADSTONE = WILD AGITATOR! MEANS WELL.

? Make up some anagrams of your own of famous people's names. Try to make your anagram say something true about the person or their work. (You will probably find it helps to write each letter of the name on a separate small piece of paper so you can move them around on a table.)

Doublets

Doublets is a game said to have been invented by Lewis Carroll. To play doublets you need two words linked in meaning, and with the same number of letters eg head and foot. You must go from the first word to the second, one move at a time, by putting in other words which change one letter only at each step. The winner is the person who uses the least number of moves. No proper names allowed! For example:

HEAD to FOOT in 5 moves	TEA to CUP in 5 moves
H E A T	P E A
B E A T	P E T
B O A T	P U T
B O O T	P U P
F O O T	C U P

? Solve these Doublets. Who can do them in the fewest moves?

DOG to SIT   POST to CARD   DAWN to DUSK   HOME to WORK

COAL to FIRE   BLACK to WHITE   ROAD to RAIL   NOSE to TAIL

Now make up some of your own and try them out on friends.

Victorian light verse

Edward Lear's self-portrait from his Book of Nonsense.

Limericks

The Limerick packs laughs anatomical
Into space that is quite economical,
But the good ones I've seen
So seldom are clean,
And the clean ones so seldom are comical.

(Anon)

Limericks were being written long before the Victorian period, but it was not until 1846, when Edward Lear published his famous *Book of Nonsense* that they became well-known. For a while, they were called 'learics', a cross between his name and the word 'lyrics'.

The form

There was a young lady of Ryde,
Who ate some green apples and died;
The apples, fermented,
Inside the lamented,
Made cider inside her inside.

(Anon)

A limerick has five lines. The first, second and fifth lines rhyme with each other, as does the third with the fourth. There is a strong regular rhythm which can be heard if you read the examples aloud. The name of a place is often included in the first line.

Limericks were written by many of the 19th century writers, including Lewis Carroll, Robert Louis Stevenson, Algernon Swinburne, Lord Tennyson and Dante Gabriel Rossetti. They often used the form to poke fun at people, or to parody Edward Lear's limericks. Look at W. S. Gilbert's reworking of Lear's limerick:

There was an Old Man in a tree,
Who was horribly stung by a bee;
When they said: 'Does it buzz?'
He replied: 'Yes, it does.
It's a regular brute of a bee!'

Edward Lear

There was an old man of St Bees
Who was horribly stung by a wasp.
When they said: 'Does it hurt?'
He replied: 'No, it doesn't –
It's a good job it wasn't a hornet!'

W. S. Gilbert

? Write your own limerick. It should be about a person from a particular place to whom something happens.

There was a .... from ....

Grues

Billy, in one of his nice new sashes,
Fell in the fire and was burnt to ashes.
Now, although the room grows chilly,
I haven't the heart to poke poor Billy.

Harry Graham

The name 'grue' is said to have been given to these rhymes by Robert Louis Stevenson. 'Grue' is an old Scottish word meaning 'to feel horror, and to shiver with fear'. It only became an accepted English word around 1850, but was soon widely used as part of the adjective 'gruesome'.

The form

Grues are short, funny rhymes of a somewhat grisly kind. They generally describe an accident or tragedy which is far from comic. A grue has four lines. The first and second lines rhyme, as do the third and fourth. There is a strong regular rhythm.

Although grues were popular, most were published anonymously because of their gruesome subjects. The best-known writer of grues was Harry Graham, who published his first book of *Ruthless Rhymes for Heartless Homes* in 1899 under the pseudonym Col. D. Streamer (because he was in the Coldstream Guards).

The Stern Parent

Father heard his children scream,
So he threw them in the stream,
Saying, as he drowned the third,
'Children should be seen not heard!'

Harry Graham

? Write your own grue. Remember a grue should be a macabre (gruesome) tale of someone suffering a dreadful fate, but told in an amusing way.

Clerihews

Sir Humphrey Davy
Detested gravy.
He lived in the odium
Of having discovered Sodium.

E. C. Bentley

Clerihews take their name from their inventor, Edmund Clerihew Bentley. Sir Humphrey Davy was his first example, written in 1890, when he was 16 years old.

The form

A clerihew is a humorous verse about a famous person, whose name appears in the first line. There are four lines which are usually of uneven length and rhythm. The first and second lines rhyme, as do the third and fourth. Clerihews are gently satirical rather than cruel.

'The moustache of Adolf Hitler
Could hardly be littler,'
Was the thought that kept recurring
To Field-Marshal Goering.

E. C. Bentley

Napoleon Bonaparte
Thought he was pretty smart;
But he really hadn't a clue
When he met his Waterloo.

S. L. B.

? Write your own clerihew. You will have to think of a person and the reason why he or she is famous.

Parodies

Literary parodies are pieces of writing (poems or prose) which copy the form of another very well-known piece in a humorous and mocking way. The best parodies are witty and cleverly written. They are a kind of exercise in playing with language and they were very popular in Victorian times. A parody only really works if the reader knows the original piece on which it is based; otherwise the joke is lost.

How doth the little busy bee
Improve each shining hour,
And gather honey all the day
From every opening flower.

How skilfully she builds her cell;
How neat she spreads the way,
And labours hard to store it well
With the sweet food she makes.

Isaac Watts

How doth the little crocodile
Improve his shining tail,
And pour the waters of the Nile
On every golden scale!

How cheerfully he seems to grin,
How neatly spread his claws,
And welcome little fishes in
With gently smiling jaws!

Lewis Carroll

Isaac Watts' poem was well known to Victorian children, so Lewis Carroll's parody (in *Alice's Adventures in Wonderland*) would have amused them greatly. Almost all of the poems in the *Alice* books are, in fact, parodies of other poems which children would probably have learnt by heart, including Jane Taylor's popular rhyme:

Twinkle, twinkle little star,
How I wonder what you are;
Up above the world so high
Like a diamond in the sky.

Jane Taylor

Twinkle, twinkle, little bat!
How I wonder that you're at!
Up above the world you fly,
Like a tea-tray in the sky.

Lewis Carroll

I found Hemlock Jones in the old Brook Street lodgings, musing before the fire – So absorbed was he even then, in tracking some mysterious clue, that he did not seem to notice me. But therein I was wrong – as I always was in my attempts to understand that powerful intellect.
'It is raining,' he said, without lifting his head.
'You have been out, then?' I said quickly.
'No. But I see that your umbrella is wet, and that your overcoat has drops of water on it.'
I sat aghast at his penetration. After a pause he said carelessly, as if dismissing the subject: 'Besides, I hear the rain on the window. Listen.'
I listened. I could scarcely credit my ears, but there was the soft pattering of drops on the panes. It was evident there was no deceiving this man!

(from *The Stolen Cigar Case* by Bret Harte)

? Compare this extract from a parody by the 19th century American writer, Bret Harte, with the extract from the first Sherlock Holmes story on page 43.

This is part of a parody of one of Tennyson's most famous poems, *The Charge of the Light Brigade*. The parody is about a church choir singing the hymn, known as *Old Hundred*, completely out of time and tune.

...Screeched all the trebles here,
Boggled the tenors there,
Raising the parson's hair,
While his mind wandered;
Theirs not to reason why
This psalm was pitched too high:
Theirs but to gasp and cry
Out the Old Hundred.

Trebles to right of them,
Tenors to left of them,
Basses in front of them,
Bellowed and thundered.
Stormed they with shout and yell,
Not wise they sang nor well,
Drowning the sexton's bell,
While all the church wondered...

Anon

The most parodied poem in the world?

I never nurs'd a dear gazelle,
To glad me with its soft black eye,
But when it came to know me well,
And love me, it was sure to die!

This poem by Thomas Moore (1778–1852) is one of the most parodied poems ever. Many writers have been unable to resist playing with it. Here are a few Victorian ones:

I never rear'd a young gazelle,
(Because, you see, I never tried);
But had it known and loved me well,
No doubt the creature would have died.

My rich and aged Uncle John
Has known me long and loves me well,
But still persists in living on –
I would he were a young gazelle....

(Henry S. Leigh, 1837–83)

I never nursed a dear Gazelle, to glad me with its soft black eye, but when it came to know me well, and love me, it was sure to marry a market-gardener.

(Charles Dickens, *The Old Curiosity Shop*)

I never had a piece of toast,
Particularly long and wide,
But fell upon the sanded floor,
And always on the buttered side.

(Anon)

I never nursed a dear gazelle,
To glad me with its dappled hide,
But, when it came to know me well,
It fell upon the buttered side.

(Thomas Hood the Younger, 1835–74)

? Write your own parody of the 'Gazelle' poem. Notice the rhyme scheme – lines 1 and 3 rhyme, as do lines 2 and 4. You must also keep to the same rhythm, unless, like Dickens, you deliberately want to play around with it.

Try writing parodies of other famous poems, songs, or rhymes. The originals might be Victorian, but could be from any era, including modern ones.

Do you know any playground rhymes which are parodies? (For example, While shepherds washed their socks by night ...) Make a collection of such rhymes. You could make a book of parodies with illustrations. Or you could record them on tape and make a radio programme about parodies and why you think people write them and enjoy reading them.

The satire of Dickens, Thackeray and Trollope

Satire is the act of mocking people and institutions, and of drawing attention to their faults through humour or sarcasm. Satire can be a very useful weapon for a writer wanting to poke fun at people and institutions. Usually the targets are members of what is known as The Establishment. These include people such as politicians, doctors, teachers, lawyers and church ministers.

The following extract attacks politicians and the way they behave:

> Then there is my Lord Boodle … He perceives … that supposing the present Government to be overthrown, the limited choice … in the formation of a new Ministry would lie between Lord Coodle and Sir Thomas Doodle … Then giving the Home Department and the Leadership of the House of Commons to Joodle, the Exchequer to Koodle, the Colonies to Loodle, and the Foreign Office to Moodle, what are you to do with Noodle? You can't offer him the Presidency of the Council; that is reserved for Poodle … That the country is shipwrecked, lost, and gone to pieces … because you can't provide for Noodle!
>
> (from *Bleak House* by Charles Dickens)

Charles Dickens

Charles Dickens cared deeply about poor and disadvantaged people. He wanted to help to change the way society was run. As a child he had known what it was like to live in poverty. For a while his father was even in the Marshalsea debtors' prison where Charles visited him. At twelve years old, he had to work in a blacking factory for 12 hours a day and 6 shillings a week wages. The rest of his family were forced to sell their belongings and move into the Marshalsea with his father. Charles had to survive on his own. He never forgot these experiences. Although his satire was usually done with humour, underneath he was making very serious criticisms.

The Civil Service has often been satirised for the amount of form-filling that goes on. Dickens made up The Circumlocution Office as the ultimate in such departments. ('Circumlocution' means using many words where one would be enough.)

> The Circumlocution Office was … the most important Department under Government … It was impossible to do the plainest right and to undo the plainest wrong without the express authority of the Circumlocution Office. If another Gunpowder Plot had been discovered half an hour before the lighting of the match, nobody would have been justified in saving the parliament until there had been half a score of boards, half a bushel of minutes, several sacks of official memoranda, and a family-vault full of ungrammatical correspondence, on the part of the Circumlocution Office … Whatever was required to be done, the Circumlocution Office was beforehand with all the public departments in the art of perceiving – HOW NOT TO DO IT.
>
> (from *Little Dorrit* by Charles Dickens)

Thackeray and Trollope

Thackeray and Trollope were both keen observers of society. They delighted in showing up people's follies and their often inflated opinions of themselves. Unlike Dickens, however, they did not want to change society, they merely wrote stories about it.

In Anthony Trollope's series of novels about Barsetshire, the main target is the church. In this extract from *Barchester Towers* several clergymen are gathered outside the room of the old dean who has had a bad stroke. Instead of worrying about him, they discuss who might replace him:

> 'He was an excellent, sweet-tempered man,' said one of the vicar's choral. 'Heaven knows how we shall repair his loss.'
> 'He was indeed,' said a minor canon;… I suppose the government will appoint … I trust we will have no stranger.'
> 'We will not talk about his successor,' said the archdeacon, 'while there is yet hope.'
> 'Oh no, of course not,' said the minor canon. 'It would be exceedingly indecorous. but–'
> 'I know of no man,' said the meagre little prebendary, 'who has better interest with the present government than Mr. Slope.'
> 'Mr. Slope,' said two or three at once… 'Mr. Slope dean of Barchester!'
> 'Pooh!' exclaimed the burly chancellor…
> The archdeacon had almost turned pale at the idea…
> 'It would certainly not be very pleasant for us to have Mr. Slope at the deanery,' said the little prebendary, chuckling inwardly at the evident consternation which his surmise had created.

In Thackeray's famous novel, *Vanity Fair*, he satirises the snobbishness of all the different layers of society, particularly the upper classes. He even wrote a whole book on Snobs which was actually popular among the very people he was satirising!

Here he enjoys making up names for those attending a society evening. It was important for a society hostess to be seen to have invited all the right people and for others to read about it in the next day's newspapers.

And the day after, there appeared among the fashionable réunions in the *Morning Post* a paragraph to the following effect:–
... 'After dinner Mrs. Crawley had an assembly, which was attended by the Duchess (Dowager) of Stilton, Duc de la Gruyère, Marchioness of Cheshire, Marchese Alessandro Strachino, Comte de Brie, Baron Shapzuger, Chevalier Tosti, Countess of Slingstone, and Lady F. Macadam, Major-General and Lady G. Macbeth, and (2) Miss Macbeths; Viscount Paddington, Sir Horace Fogey, Hon. Sands Bedwin, Bobbachy Bahawder,'...

(from *Vanity Fair* by William Makepeace Thackeray)

? One of the devices of satire used by all three of these authors was to invent incredible names which often summed up the characters. Can you match some of their names to the descriptions of the people?

Mr and Mrs Lookaloft; Dr Fillgrave; Mr M'Choakumchild; Mr Vellem Deeds; Mr Gusher; Dr Swishtail; Mrs Mantrap; Dr Rerechild; Capt Deuceace; Mr Quiverful; Earl and Lady Castlemouldy; Mr Tangle and Mr Snagsby

(an attorney; two members of the legal profession; a gambling soldier; a public speaker; a doctor; a schoolmaster disciplinarian; a children's doctor; an attractive woman; an unimaginative schoolmaster; a minor clergyman with 14 children; a pair of social climbers; two members of the old aristocracy)

Make up names for members of modern professions or types of people. The names can be as outrageous as you like but must tell us something about the people, for example Mr Bentley Toocars and Miss Pansy Flutterlid.

Dotheboys Hall, the school run by Wackford Squeers in Nicholas Nickleby.

Theatres and dream palaces

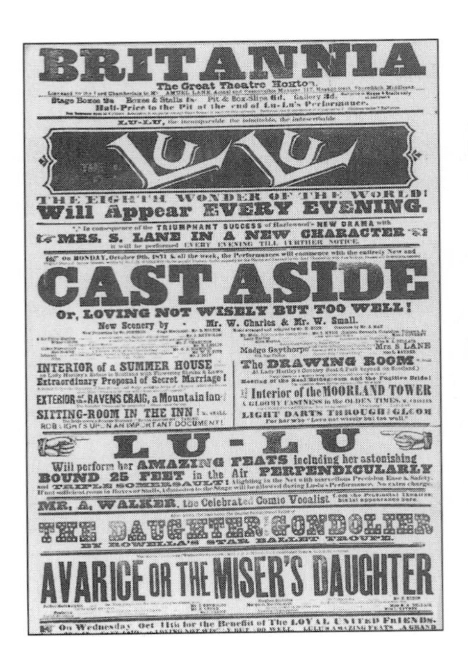

Dream palaces

> In the nineties what playgoer worth his salt would willingly miss the Britannia pantomime in which the septuagenarian (70 year-old) Sara Lane would play the principal boy with all the bravery of tights and trunks to the delight of the gallery boys who worshipped her? Few restaurants got rid of so much solid food as the Britannia audience would consume during five or six hours dramatic debauch. Men walked to and fro incessantly with trays groaning beneath the weight of pies in infinite variety, thick slices of bread plastered with jam, chunks of cheese, slabby sandwiches, fried fish, jellied eels. Gallons of ale washed down mountains of food.
>
> (from *Fifty Years of a Londoner's Life* by H. G. Hibbert)

The most popular theatres at this time were like the Britannia in Hoxton, London, offering a mix of pantomime, melodrama and variety acts. They were a favourite night out for ordinary people, as well as some of the better off. In *London Labour and the London Poor,* Henry Mayhew recorded what an intelligent working class costermonger (a street-stall seller) said:

> Love and murder suits us best sir; but within these few years I think there's a great deal more liking for deep tragedies among us. They set men a'thinking but then we all consider them too long. Of Hamlet we can make neither end nor side; and nine out of ten of us – ay far more than that – would like it to be confined to the ghost scenes, and the funeral, and the killing off at the last. Macbeth would be better liked, if it was only the witches and the fighting – We always stay to the last, because we've paid for it all … We are fond of music … Flash songs are liked, and sailors' songs and patriotic songs.

Music Hall created superstars, such as George Leybourne.

Victorian melodrama

One of the most popular forms of theatre was the melodrama. Melodramas were sensational and emotional, fast-moving stories whose main elements were love and murder. There would also be short comic interludes.

The stock characters were the:

HERO; VILLAIN; HEROINE; AN OLD MAN; AN OLD WOMAN; A COMIC MAN AND A COMIC WOMAN

Heroes were noble, strong and upright, but not very bright. They were cheered by audiences. Villains were wicked, clever, fascinating, and outwitted the hero during most of the play. They were hissed and booed. The lovely heroine always swooned, and had to be rescued by the hero from the evil clutches of the villain. In the end, though, Good triumphs over Evil.

During these playlets, music was very important – for example, a violin played at a crucial moment for the heroine to tug at the audience's heartstrings, and urgent, lively music could create tension for a chase, a fight or an oncoming train. Not only was music used, but also stage lighting, machinery and sound effects. Among these, rolling thunder, wind and rain machines and trap doors all contributed to an exciting evening out.

A poster for the melodrama, The Whip, *directed by Sensation Smith at Drury Lane, during which a train crash actually took place on stage!*

?

Write a short melodrama with some friends. Remind yourselves of the necessary ingredients for such a melodrama and make a storyboard series of pictures for the main scenes. Decide on the characters and give them names. Write the dialogue and plan what sound and other effects you will use. You could also make a tape of appropriate music to play at different moments. Remember, these melodramas were high tragedy with comic moments, and were not particularly realistic. There should be plenty of action and nail-biting incidents, as well as moments of tear-jerking sorrow.

Rehearse your play and then perform it to others.

A poster for Irving's Faust *at the Lyceum.*

Straight Theatre

At the beginning of the period, actors and, particularly actresses, were thought a loose-living and disreputable lot. So, going to the theatre was not an entirely respectable thing for the well-off classes to do. Queen Victoria's love of theatre, however, helped to change this and by the end of the century serious theatre was flourishing again.

This was the time of great Actor-Managers, such as Henry Irving and Herbert Beerbohm Tree. Irving was obviously a very talented actor who thrilled audiences at the Lyceum in the West End of London which he ran from 1878 to 1899. With his leading lady, Ellen Terry, he dominated serious theatre during this time, notably with his productions of Shakespeare, and was the first actor ever to receive a knighthood. He famously used all sorts of lighting effects and was the first to dim the house lights during a performance. Before then, house lights had stayed on and audiences would chatter all through plays unless something grabbed their attention!

Gilbert and Sullivan

W S Gilbert wrote the words for fourteen comic operas, which contain many witty songs making fun of different aspects of society. These were set to music by Arthur Sullivan and are known as the Savoy operas, after the theatre which was built especially for their performances. Among their best-known operas are *The Mikado, HMS Pinafore,* and *The Pirates of Penzance*.

In *The Mikado*, Ko-Ko, The Lord High Executioner, sings about all the people who irritate him and whom he would like to execute. The song begins:

As someday it may happen that a victim must be found,
I've got a little list – I've got a little list
Of society offenders who might well be underground,
And who never would be missed – who never would be missed!

He continues in rhyming couplets to list such people; for example:

There's the pestilential nuisances who write for autographs –
All people who have flabby hands and irritating laughs –

And ends –

They'd none of 'em be missed - they'd none of 'em be missed.

Beginning with the same four lines, make up your own list of all the kinds of people who irritate you. You must stick to the same rhythm and rhyme scheme – rhyming couplets – and end with the same line as Gilbert's. For example:

There's the ones who always think they're better than the rest of us,
And those who when they cut themselves must always make a fuss,
And all who barge in front of you to push into the queue,
And people sneezing in your face when they have got the 'flu …

Oscar Wilde (1854–1900) was the leading Victorian playwright. His best known play is The Importance of Being Earnest.

Victorian toys

Penny Plain, Twopence Coloured

Dr Henry Danson was a school friend of Charles Dickens. Here he is remembering how they used to enjoy playing with toy theatres:

> We mounted small theatres and got up very gorgeous scenery to illustrate *The Miller and his Men* and *Cherry and Fair Star* [both popular plays]. I remember the present Mr Beverly, the scene painter, assisted us in this. Dickens was always the leader in these plays, which were occasionally presented with much solemnity before an audience of boys in the presence of the ushers. My brother, assisted by Dickens, got up *The Miller and his Men* in a very gorgeous form. Master Beverly constructed the mill for us in such a way that it could tumble to pieces with the assistance of crackers. At one representation the fireworks in the last scene ending with the destruction of the mill were so very real that the police interfered and knocked violently at the doors.

Cut-out characters for a toy theatre.

Part of a printed sheet for a toy theatre.

Toy theatres were very popular amongst children. Sheets of characters from favourite melodramas were printed and sold at 1d for those which you coloured yourself, and 2d for already coloured ones. The small figures, based on well-known actors, were cut out and fixed to little sticks so they could be moved on the small stage. The theatres often came with footlights in which oil was burned, and there was an orchestra pit with players painted along the bottom of the stage.

? Draw your own cut-out characters for a play, pantomime or film.

Cinematic toys

Early cinema began with simple experiments in making pictures seem to move. A very popular toy, for both adults and children, was the zoetrope. Strips of card were placed round the inside of a metal drum which had slits running down from the top edge. The strips had a series of pictures of the same thing. However, each picture showed the object in a slightly different position. When the drum was spun round and you looked through the slits, the object appeared to move.

A zoetrope

Movie films work on the same basic principle. Each separate frame of a film is a still picture. When the frames are projected at speed, the frames pass so quickly in front of the eye that the images seem to move.

A Thaumatrope

With your compasses, draw a circle, radius 3cm, onto card.

Cut out the circle. On one side of the circle draw the outline of a bird cage.

On the other side, draw a bird – **the bird should be the other way up from the cage**. Make a small hole on each side of the circle. Thread some thin string through and knot it carefully. Hold the strings in each hand and twist them backwards and forwards. The bird should appear to be in the cage.

> **?** Make up some different ideas for pictures and try them out; for example:
>
> - Horse one side, jockey the other
> - Cat and tree
> - Car and road

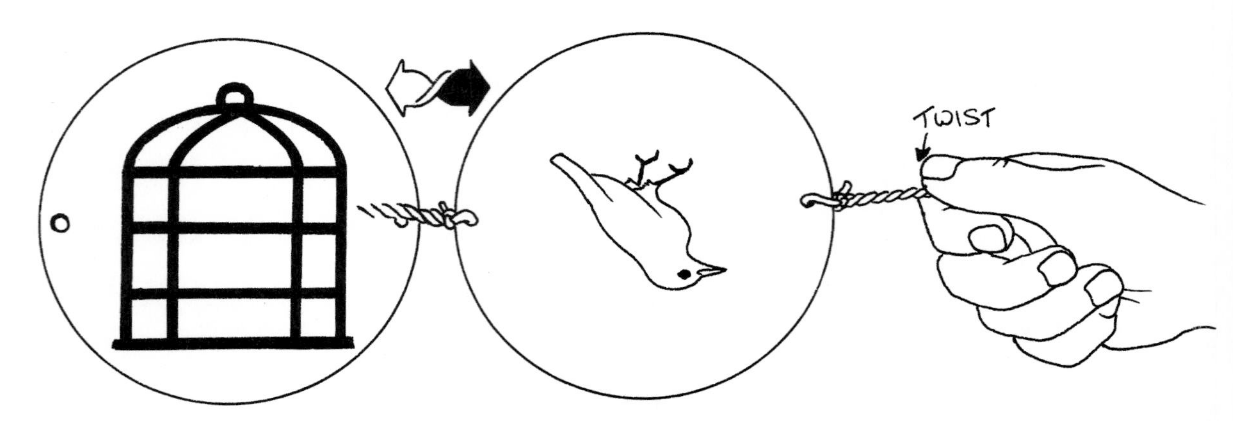

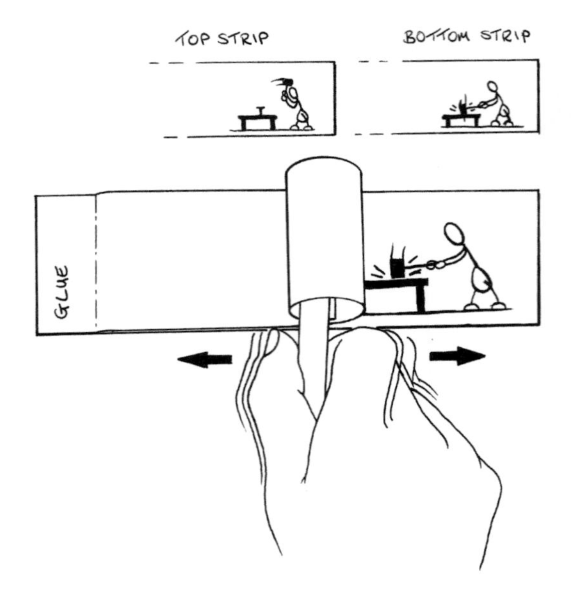

Simple moving picture

Stick two strips of paper together at one end. At the other end, on the top piece, draw a simple picture. Press hard so that it leaves an impression on the strip below. On the second piece, trace over the impression but make one alteration. Place the strips flat on a table and curl the end of the top piece round a pencil. Run the pencil backwards and forwards so that you see both pictures alternately. They should appear to move.

A flicker book

Cut 20 identical rectangles of paper (5cm x 7cm). Stick them together at one end and then tape right round that end.

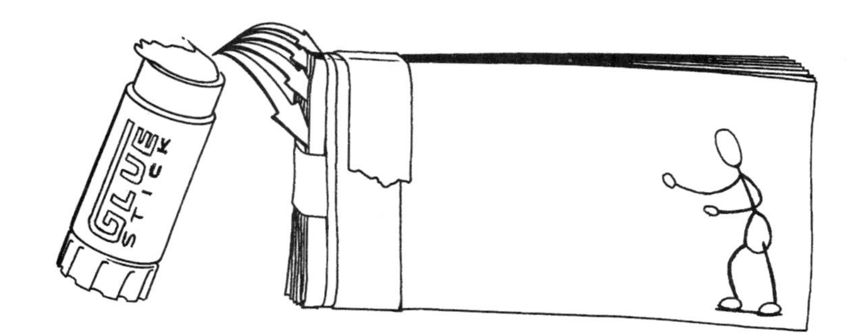

To the right of the first sheet, draw a simple picture of a person or animal – if you are not very good at drawing, pin men or animals are easiest!

Press quite hard so that the impression of your picture shows through on each new sheet. Now, on the next, draw over the impression of your picture but make a slight difference. Do this each time until you have completed all the sheets.

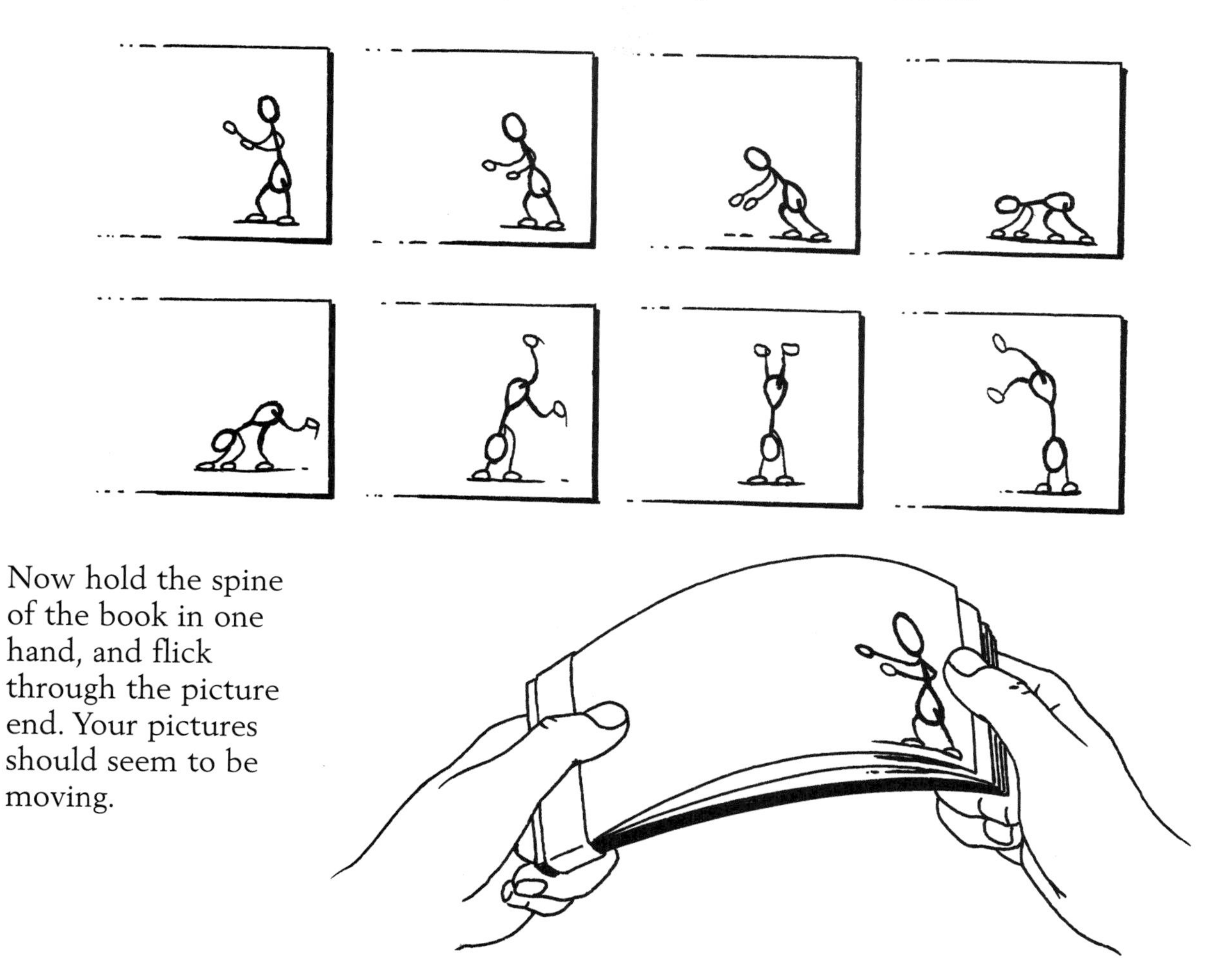

Now hold the spine of the book in one hand, and flick through the picture end. Your pictures should seem to be moving.

Children's books

Alice with Turtle and Gryphon

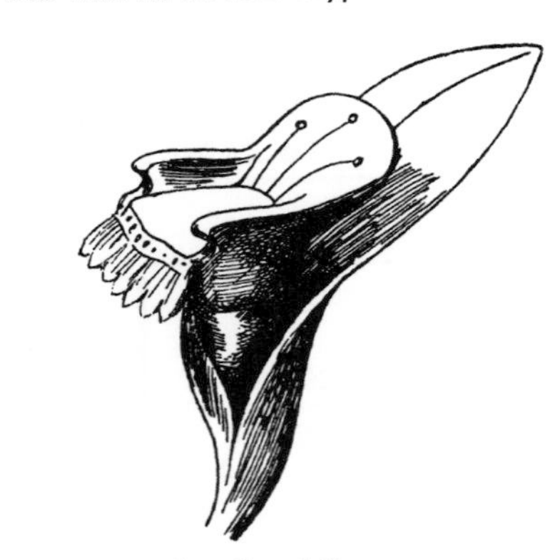

Armchairia Comfortabilis

A new kind of writing

To the Looking-Glass world it was Alice that said,
'I've a sceptre in hand, I've a crown on my head;
Let the Looking-Glass creatures, whatever they be,
Come and dine with the Red Queen, the White Queen, and me!
Then fill up the glasses as quick as you can,
And sprinkle the table with buttons and bran:
Put cats in the coffee, and mice in the tea –
And welcome Queen Alice with thirty-times-three!

(From *Through the Looking-Glass* by Lewis Carroll)

The 19th century was the first time that books were really written for children's entertainment, rather than to educate them or teach them to be good. Several writers, such as Charles Kingsley in his *Water Babies*, still produced books whose main aim was to improve behaviour and make good future citizens; this was one of the attitudes we have come to think of as typically Victorian. However, even these books usually had interesting storylines.

But a new kind of writing was emerging. Neither Edward Lear nor Lewis Carroll was interested in telling children how to behave. Their writing was for fun, or to ridicule or send up the grown-up world in various ways (something which always appeals to children). Can you think of any authors or poets today who have a similar approach?

Bubblia Blowpipia *'Botany' from Lear's* Book of Nonsense.

Books from Europe and America

There were some very good books, written for children in other countries, which were immediately successful when they were published in Britain. They must have influenced and encouraged English writers (and readers) and helped the spread of more interesting children's books. See the box below for some of these books.

What do you notice about the books listed? Are they titles that you know? Choose one book from the box and discuss why you think it is still popular today.

Do you think that there are any modern children's books which will be read and enjoyed by children in 100 years' time? If so, which ones might they be?

The Brothers Grimm (Germany) – their fairy tales came out in translation in the 1820s.

Hans Christian Andersen, his Danish fairy tales came out in translation in the 1840s.

Mark Twain (USA) *The Adventures of Tom Sawyer* (1876).

Louisa May Alcott (USA) *Little Women* (1868).

Harriet Beecher Stowe (USA) *Uncle Tom's Cabin* (1851).

Susan Coolidge (USA) *What Katy Did* (1871).

Joel Chandler Harris (USA) *Uncle Remus Stories* (1880).

Johanna Spyri (Switzerland) *Heidi* (transl. 1884).

L. Frank Baum (USA) *The Wonderful Wizard of Oz* (1900).

School stories

School stories really started during the Victorian era. They found a ready market among the children of the new middle classes who were being sent away to school, and among others who were benefiting from the move towards schooling for everyone. Although there had been a few school stories before, it was Thomas Hughes' *Tom Brown's Schooldays* (1857), about Rugby School, which made this new type of writing popular.

School stories then appeared in cheap magazines for boys. These papers were known as 'penny-dreadfuls' which gives an idea of the level of the writing in them! A new quality penny magazine, *The Boy's Own Paper*, was launched in 1879. It was here that the famous story, *The Fifth Form at St Dominic's*, by Talbot Baines Reed, was first printed as a serial. Soon girls' stories also began to be published, as more girls were allowed to be educated at school.

No. 1.—Vol. I. SATURDAY, JANUARY 18, 1879. Price One Penny. [ALL RIGHTS RESERVED.

MY FIRST FOOTBALL MATCH.

BY AN OLD BOY.

IT was a proud moment in my existence when Wright, captain of our football club, came up to me in school one Friday and said, "Adams, your name is down to play in the match against Craven to-morrow."

I could have knighted him on the spot. To be one of the picked "fifteen," whose glory it was to fight the battles of their school in the Great Close, had been the leading ambition of my life—I suppose I ought to be ashamed to confess it—ever since, as a little chap of ten, I entered Parkhurst six years ago. Not a winter Saturday but had seen me either looking on at some big match, or oftener still scrimmaging about with a score or so of other juniors in a scratch game. But for a long time, do what I would, I always seemed as far as ever from the coveted goal, and was half despairing of ever rising to win my "first fifteen cap." Latterly, however, I had noticed Wright and a few others of our best players more than once lounging about in the Little Close where we juniors used to play, evidently taking observations with an eye to business. Under the awful gaze of these heroes, need I say I exerted myself as I had never done before? What cared I for hacks or bruises, so only that I could distinguish myself in their eyes? And never was music sweeter

"Down!"

Adventure Stories

Fifteen men on The Dead Man's Chest –
Yo-ho-ho, and a bottle of rum!
Drink and the devil had done for the rest –
Yo-ho-ho, and a bottle of rum!

Pirates, smugglers, shipwrecks, desert islands and buried treasure – these were the elements in two of the best adventure stories of Victorian times – *Treasure Island*, by Robert Louis Stevenson, and *Moonfleet*, by J Meade Falkner. Both tales are wonderfully exciting and have young heroes who appeal to children. Jim Hawkins sets sail for Treasure Island as cabin boy aboard the *Hispaniola* with a crew of pirates who mutiny. Their leader, the one-legged Long John Silver, with his talking parrot ('pieces of eight!'), has become one of the most famous characters in children's literature. In *Moonfleet*, John Trenchard becomes involved with smugglers and embarks on an adventure which includes the finding of Blackbeard's cursed treasure in the well of Carisbrooke Castle:

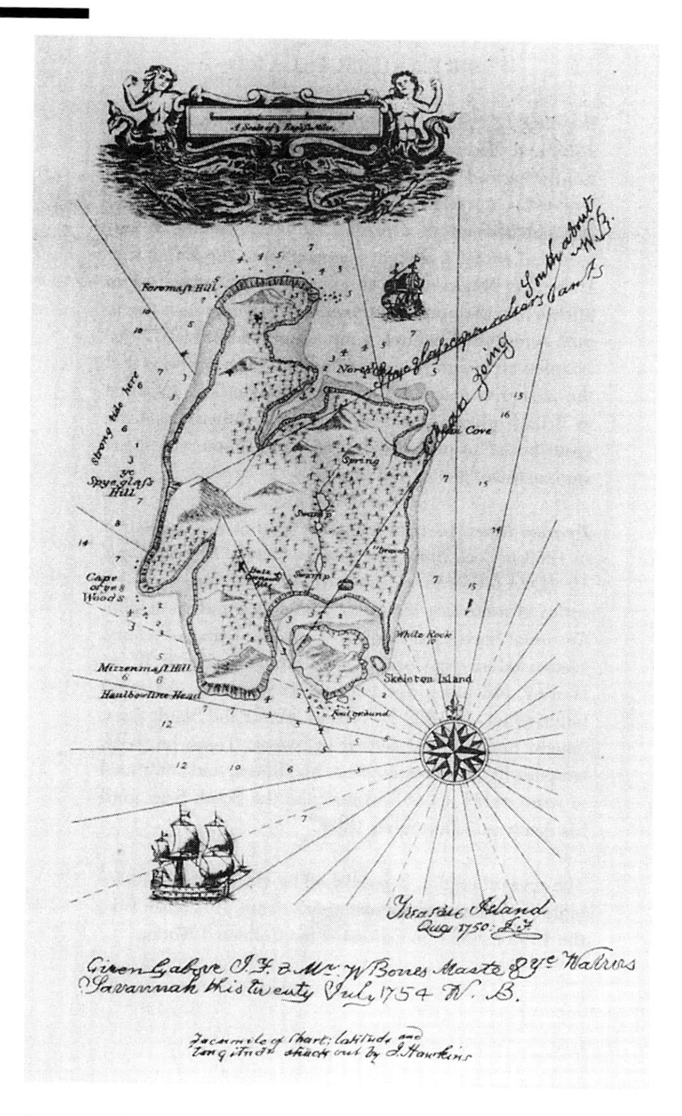

Stevenson's map for Treasure Island.

> 'Yes,' I shouted back, 'I have found the treasure; you can pull me up.' The words were scarcely out of my mouth before the bucket began to move, and I went up a great deal faster than I had gone down. Yet in that short journey other thoughts came to my mind, and I heard Grace's voice again, sweet and grave, 'Have a care, have a care how you touch the treasure; it was evilly come by, and will bring a curse with it.'
>
> (from *Moonfleet*, 1898, by J Meade Falkner)

Although most of the adventure stories were written by men and intended for boys, girls, of course, also read them. In time, as women and girls had more access to education and they began to lead fuller lives, girls also became more central in children's books.

Early adventure books

The first Victorian adventure books began with the stories of Captain Marryat, particularly *Masterman Ready* (1841) and *The Children of the New Forest* (1847). Before Stevenson's highly successful books in the 1880s, which also included *Kidnapped* and *The Black Arrow*, probably the best were by R M Ballantyne. His most famous is *Coral Island*, published in 1857. The story is about three boys, Ralph, Jack and Peterkin, who are shipwrecked on a coral island. Through the narrator, Ralph, we hear how they manage to survive, and about their adventures, which include encounters with pirates and savages. William Golding based his 20th century story, *Lord of the Flies*, on *Coral Island*. However, his version shows the shipwrecked boys behaving very differently from Ballantyne's.

Make up, and write down, the outline of an adventure story which results in the finding of some treasure. *Do not write the story.*

Here are some questions to help you with your planning:

Who is telling the story? Who is the hero/heroine? What other characters are in the story? Where does it take place? What is the treasure – gold, money, jewels, or something quite different from these? Where is the treasure? Who knew that there was treasure to be found? How is it discovered? What problems are there along the way?

Now write the episode in which the treasure is actually found. As this comes late on you will have to have thought about all the above questions so you know the back story (what has gone before). It might help to write some short descriptions of the main characters so that you understand how they think and how they might react in the situation.

More Victorian parlour games

Yes and No

It was a Game called Yes and No, where Scrooge's nephew had to think of something, and the rest must find out what; he only answering to their questions 'yes' or 'no' as the case was. The brisk fire of questioning to which he was exposed, elicited from him that he was thinking of an animal, a live animal, rather a disagreeable animal, a savage animal, an animal that growled and grunted sometimes, and talked sometimes, and lived in London, and walked about the streets, and wasn't made a show of, and wasn't led by anyone, and didn't live in a menagerie, and was never killed in a market, and was not a horse, or an ass, or a cow, or a bull, or a tiger, or a dog, or a pig, or a cat, or a bear. At every fresh question that was put to him, this nephew burst into a fresh roar of laughter; and was so inexpressibly tickled, that he was obliged to get up off the sofa and stamp. At last the plump sister, falling into a similar state, cried out:

'I have found it out! I know what it is, Fred! I know what it is!'

'What is it?' cried Fred.

'It's your Uncle Scro-o-o-o-oge!'

Which it certainly was…

(from *A Christmas Carol*, Charles Dickens)

? Play 'Yes and No' with your friends (it is similar to 20 Questions). Make your subjects characters from novels you have all been reading. Or choose characters from one book you all know (for example, *Oliver Twist*, or *Alice in Wonderland*).

The Minister's Cat (also The Parson's Cat and The Vicar's Cat)

These rules are from *Games for Parlour and Playground* (1898) by A B Gomme:

> The first player begins by saying, 'The parson's cat is an ambitious cat', the next player 'an affable cat', the next 'an amiable cat', and so on, until they have all named an adjective beginning with A. The next time of going round the adjectives must begin with B, the next time C, and so on, until the whole of the alphabet, or as much of it as is possible, has been gone through. The game is made more difficult and more interesting by each player having to repeat what the previous players have said, and then adding his or her own contribution.

? Play the Minister's (Parson's/Vicar's) Cat the way Victorians played it. Remember each person must say a *different* adjective beginning with each different letter of the alphabet. Naturally, if you cannot think of a different one you are out! If a different person begins each letter round, this would ensure that the same person is not always at the end! If your group is not too large, you might like to play in the way suggested in the rules above where you repeat all the other adjectives. For example:

(1st) The vicar's cat is a big cat.

(2nd) The vicar's cat is a big, bold cat.

(3rd) The vicar's cat is a big, bold, brave cat.

(4th) The vicar's cat is a big, bold, brave, boss-eyed cat –

Start afresh with C.

Words within words

In this game, sometimes just called 'Words', players have to make as many different words as possible out of the letters of a given word. For example, from **words** you can come up with the following:

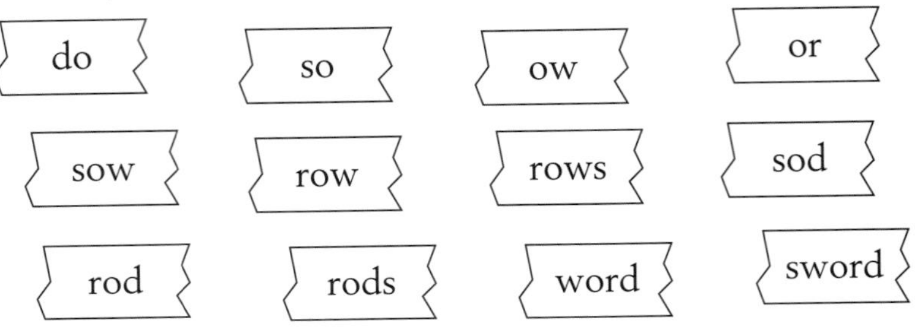

The winner is the person who finds the greatest number.

Charades

The popular pastime, Charades, was originally a written game. It was during the Victorian period that the game changed to one still played today in various versions. The object of the game was for people to guess a word which was acted out by a small group. The word was divided either into syllables or longer parts, and each part was acted out in a little scene. The whole word formed the final scene. Sometimes the scenes were just mimed, sometimes the syllables, and then the whole word, were hidden within the dialogue. For example: 'servant' might break down into 'serve' and 'ant'. The first scene might show someone serving food – any dialogue might include the line, 'Waiter! Waiter! Is there anyone here to serve me?' The second scene might be a visit to a natural history museum – any dialogue might include, 'And here we see the honey bee, wood ant, and stag beetle in their natural habitats'. The final scene might show someone ordering a friend to do all sorts of things – dialogue might include, 'Get it yourself! What did your last servant die of!'

?

Play charades with your friends. Here are some words you might want to use, or, better still, find some of your own. Plan your scenes to be like little stories in themselves and not to be too short. You can lay a false trail by putting in many other possible words to confuse the audience!

mis(s)-taken car-nation his-tory friend-ship Germ-any Liver-pool pot-a-toes Vic-tor-ian under-stand-able pa-nora-ma in-term-in-able

?

The 1872 *Chamber's Journal* says that 61 words can be made from the letters in the word 'Cambridge'. How many can you find? You might find it helps to write the letters on small pieces of paper so that you can move them around on the table to create new words.

The same journal also claims that there are 170 words to be found from the letters of 'handkerchief'! Can you find them all?

Letters

Letters are very fascinating and useful social documents. By studying the text of letters we can use our detective powers to find out many things of interest.

In 1890 Robert Louis Stevenson (1850–94) moved to live in Samoa in the South Pacific. From Samoa he wrote letters to many people, including other writers, such as J M Barrie and Henry James, commenting on their latest work. This letter to his fellow Scot, the writer Arthur Conan Doyle, was written in 1893, a year before Stevenson died of a brain haemorrhage.

Vailima,
July 12 1893

My Dear Dr Conan Doyle,
– The White Company [published 1891] *has not yet turned up; but when it does – which I suppose will be next mail – you shall hear news of me. I have a great talent for compliment, accompanied by a hateful, even diabolic frankness.*

Delighted to hear I have a chance of seeing you and Mrs Doyle; Mrs Stevenson bids me say (what is too true) that our rations are often spare. Are you Great Eaters? Please reply.

As to ways and means, here is what you will have to do. Leave San Francisco by the down mail, get off at Samoa, and twelve days or a fortnight later, you can continue your journey to Auckland per Upolu, which will give you a look at Tonga and possibly Fiji by the way. Make this a first part of your plans. A fortnight, even of Vailima diet, could kill nobody.

We are in the midst of war here; rather a nasty business, with the head-taking; and there seems signs of other trouble. But I believe you need make no change in your design to visit us. All should be well over; and if it were not, why! you need not leave the steamer. –

Yours very truly,
Robert Louis Stevenson

? Look at his style of writing and see if you can work out what kind of person Stevenson was. Would you say this was a formal letter? What do you imagine his life was like in Samoa? What clues are you using to support your ideas? If you had been Conan Doyle, what would you have made of this letter?

The following letter was printed in *The Times* on 5 July 1849. It had 54 signatures.

Sur,

May we beg and beseech your proteckshion and power. We are Sur, as it may be, living in a Wilderniss, so far as the rest of London knows anything of us, or as rich and great people care about. We live in muck and filthe. We aint got no privez, no dust bins, no drains, no water splies, and no drain or suer in the whole place. The Suer Company, in Greek Street, Soho Square, all great, rich and powerfool men, take no notice watsomdever of our complaints. The Stenche of a Gully-hole is disgustin. We al of us suffer, and numbers are ill, and if the Colera comes Lord help us.

What can you find out from reading this letter? Describe what you think the lives of these people were like. Why were they writing to *The Times*? What sort of person do you think wrote the letter? Does the fact that 54 people signed the letter suggest anything of particular interest?

Compare the above letter with another in *The Times* on 15 January 1864:

Sir,

I live with thousands of others down the Mid Kent Railway below Beckenham, ten miles from London Bridge, all of us requiring to be in town more or less punctually every morning. The recent 'facilities of new lines', as the phrase goes, have only woefully obstructed our business journeyings, and made our homes practically now twenty miles off London. I arrived at the London Bridge Station this evening to go home by the train appointed in the railway bills to start at 6.15; and found our train had taken a trip to Charing Cross, leaving 200 or 300 of us waiting about 15 or 20 minutes on a very unsafe, cold, exposed, narrow platform, kicking our heels about while engines and trains passed to and fro, like Cheapside omnibuses, in dangerous proximity; and after undergoing one hour and five minutes from the time our train should have started, in making a journey of ten miles.

The oldest Victorian pillar box is in St Peter Port, Guernsey. It was installed in 1853 on the orders of the novelist, Anthony Trollope, who worked for the Post Office, and is still in use.

What is this person writing about and what kind of letter is it? What kind of person do you think wrote the letter? How would the life of this writer have differed from the people writing from Soho? What clues are there in these letters, both in their written style and in what the writers say, which can help you form your opinions?

Horror and the supernatural

Dracula or the Undead

Lucy has become a vampire, one of the undead. In daylight she is in her coffin.

The lips were red, nay redder than before; and on the cheeks was a delicate bloom…
'Are you convinced now?' said the Professor…and in a way that made me shudder, pulled back the dead lips and showed the white teeth. 'See,' he went on, 'see, they are even sharper than before. With this and this' – and he touched one of the canine teeth and that below it – 'the little children can be bitten.'…
[Arthur] took the stake and the hammer, and when once his mind was set on action his hands never trembled nor even quivered … [He] placed the point over the heart, and as I looked I could see its dint in the white flesh. Then he struck with all his might. The Thing in the coffin writhed; and a hideous, blood-curdling screech came from the opened red lips… There in the coffin lay no longer the foul Thing that we had so dreaded and grown to hate …but Lucy as we had seen her in her life, with her face of unequalled sweetness and purity.

The idea for the story of Dracula began in a nightmare in 1890 for its author, Bram Stoker. Seven years later, after researching tales of vampires, he finally published the now famous story. It is set partly in Transylvania (in modern Romania), a country he never visited – all his information was taken from travel books.

Bram Stoker transformed this real figure into Count Dracula, one of the Undead, who sucked blood by night and fled into his coffin during daylight hours. Anyone bitten on the neck by Dracula or one of his maidens also turned into a vampire. The only sure way to get rid of a vampire was to drive a stake into the heart.

Since its publication, Dracula has become one of the best-known stories throughout the world. Over 200 films have been made, as well as many cartoons and comic characters created, based on the Count.

The original Vlad Dracul was a strong medieval ruler who led successful and bloody campaigns against the Turks. 'Dracul' means 'the devil'.

Dr Jekyll and Mr Hyde

> 'I had long since prepared my tincture;… and late one accursed night, I compounded the elements, watched them boil and smoke together in the glass, and … drank off the potion. The most racking pains succeeded: a grinding in the bones, deadly nausea, and a horror of the spirit that cannot be exceeded at the hour of birth or death … I knew myself, at the first breath of this new life, to be more wicked, tenfold more wicked, sold a slave to my original evil … I saw for the first time the appearance of Mr Hyde … The evil side of my nature, to which I had now transferred … was less robust and less developed than the good which I had just deposed … Edward Hyde was so much smaller, slighter, and younger than Henry Jekyll … Even as good shone upon the countenance of the one, evil was written broadly and plainly on the face of the other.'
>
> (from *The Strange Case of Dr Jekyll and Mr Hyde* by Robert Louis Stevenson)

Thus it was that Dr Jekyll began his experiment and unleashed the beast inside him in the guise of Mr Hyde, an evil murderer. Eventually he is unable to control when Mr Hyde will appear. The other side of his personality has taken him over.

> 'It was the hand of Edward Hyde … terror woke up in my breast as sudden and startling as the crash of cymbals … I rushed to the mirror. At the sight that met my eyes, my blood was changed into something exquisitely thin and icy. Yes, I had gone to bed Henry Jekyll, I had awakened Edward Hyde. How was this to be explained? I asked myself; and then, with another bound of terror – how was it to be remedied?'

This famous story about split personality came to Robert Louis Stevenson in a nightmare, too. For three days he wrote furiously, thirty thousand words in all. Then, feeling it was not right, he threw the manuscript on the fire. Over the next days he rewrote what has become one of the best known horror stories of all time. When it was published in 1886 as a 'shilling shocker', it was immediately successful. The timing of its publication meant that it soon became linked in the public's mind with the real-life murderer, Jack the Ripper (see page 41).

> ? Imagine a nightmare that could be used as the inspiration for a horror story. Try to write the opening paragraphs of the story, or draw a storyboard for the first few scenes.

Ghost stories

Scrooge sees the first of four ghosts in Charles Dickens' *A Christmas Carol*:

> It was not in impenetrable shadow as the other objects in the yard were, but had a dismal light about it, like a bad lobster in a dark cellar. It was not angry or ferocious, but looked at Scrooge as Marley used to look: with ghostly spectacles turned up upon its ghostly forehead. The hair was curiously stirred, as if by breath or hot-air; and though the eyes were wide open, they were perfectly motionless. That, and its livid colour, made it horrible...

Victorian readers loved ghost stories. Sometimes these were about ghosts of dead people coming back to haunt the living, as Jacob Marley does to Scrooge. However, the other three ghosts in this story, of Christmases Past, Present and Future, are figures that touch Scrooge's conscience and help to change him for the better. Dickens' most famous short ghost story, *The Signalman*, tells of a ghostly warning of coming doom. Yet the end of the tale suggests that something even stranger may have happened.

Doctors in the 19th century became very interested in the study of the mind. If a person's mind is affected, perhaps through a bad conscience, repressed emotions, or a terrifying experience, they can go mad and imagine all sorts of things. Some of the best stories of the supernatural can leave you wondering if the events really happened or whether they were just imagined.

? Write a short supernatural story where things are perhaps not what they seem.

Decide on a main character and choose a setting/place for the story. The main character may see or hear things. Why is s/he haunted by these? What do these visions/voices do or say? How do they affect the character? Are other people aware of them? How and when do these things appear? Do they change or get worse? What does the character do about them? What happens in the end?

Magazines

During the Victorian era magazine publishing flourished. Estimates for the year 1864 suggest that just under 2.5 million journals appeared every week, and another 2.5 million every month. Many of these were religious or educational. However, there were some literary and artistic magazines as well as those specifically for women and families. Of course, there was also the popular *Police Gazette* with its picture stories of current crimes (see page 40).

THE BEST-KNOWN LITERARY MAGAZINES

Ainsworth's Magazine, edited by W Harrison Ainsworth, a popular historical novelist.

All the Year Round and *Household Words*, both edited by Charles Dickens.

Cornhill Magazine, edited for a while by William Makepeace Thackeray.

Strand Magazine, famous for publishing short fiction, particularly the *Sherlock Holmes* stories. It also contained articles on royalty and celebrities, natural history, puzzles, cartoons, and oddities (see 'A Crocodile Story' on page 90).

Punch, an extremely popular magazine which satirised politics and society.

Work by the most famous authors of the time was often first published in instalments in magazines and made the writers into wealthy celebrities. The list includes Dickens, Trollope, Thackeray, George Eliot, Elizabeth Gaskell, Wilkie Collins, Thomas Hardy, Charlotte Brontë, Tennyson and Elizabeth Barrett Browning. They were very popular with people from all classes who would eagerly await the next instalment, even if it meant buying the magazine for as many as 20 months (as in the case of Thackeray's *Vanity Fair*) in order to find out what happened. Is there anything similar that popularises novels and writers today?

Look at 'A Crocodile Story', below, from *Strand Magazine*, 1893. What story is this comic strip telling? Is it making any deeper point about Victorian life and the Empire?

A CROCODILE STORY

Satin prints were often given free with magazines. This one came with the Christmas issue of *The Gentlewoman*, 1897. Who do you think paid the cost of producing these prints? What sort of things are given free with modern magazines? For what reasons is this done?

Comic strips are similar to storyboards for short films. Each picture tells the next part of a story and storyboards are used to plan the course of a film.

Draw a storyboard in six frames for a short film. It might be about a book, or scene from a book, you have read, such as *Alice's Adventures in Wonderland* or *Oliver Twist*. It might also be for a film of a poem, such as *The Owl and the Pussy-cat* by Edward Lear, or *The Pied Piper of Hamelin* by Robert Browning. Each square/frame will show the next important part of the story. You could also try storyboards for two 20th century story poems (by writers actually born in Victorian times): *Flannan Isle* by W. W. Gibson (1878–1962), and *The Highwayman* by Alfred Noyes (1880–1958).

Newspapers

A Bryant and May matchbox

Captain Webb makes the first successful attempt to swim the English Channel.

... After a few more strokes the brave Matthew Webb stood upright in five feet of water on Calais sands abreast of the bathing establishment and half a mile to the westward of Calais pier at 10.40.15 a.m. English time on Wednesday 25 August 1875, after having been in the water twenty-one hours forty-four minutes and fifty-five seconds without touching artificial support of any kind, and having swum as nearly as possible over thirty-nine miles and a half of ground ...

From an on-the-spot report for *The Country Gentleman's Newspaper* (1875)

During the 19th century the number of newspapers grew enormously and their circulation increased throughout the country.

W H Smith introduced the first newspaper trains to distribute papers all over Britain.

Some of the newspapers did not survive as there was great competition. However, many did. *The Times,* which had begun in 1785 as the *Daily Universal Register,* dominated the first part of the century, partly because of its excellent foreign news reporting. Enterprising people even placed advertisements in local papers offering to hire out copies of *The Times* 'On the day of Publication, at One Penny per hour: the following day, three hours for One Penny'. Later, it faced stiff competition from the *Daily News,* a Liberal paper, and the Conservative *Daily Telegraph*. Many now famous regional newspapers, such as the *Manchester Guardian,* the *Liverpool Daily Post,* and *The Scotsman* became daily papers for the first time. Where once newspapers had often been only weekly, now papers even appeared on Sundays. Two of these, *The News of the World* (first published 1843) and *The People* (1881), survive to this day.

THE NEWS OF THE WORLD.
(FIRST EDITION.)

LONDON:
SUNDAY, OCTOBER 1, 1843.

TO THE PUBLIC.

A Few Words of Introduction.

We present to the Public, A NOVELTY IN NEWSPAPER LITERATURE — *a Weekly Journal of* the Largest Size, unexampled in point of Cheapness, *and which, we trust, will be pronounced of* the highest order of merit. *Our object is to establish* A FIRST CLASS JOURNAL *at a Price which shall place it within the reach of* ALL CLASSES OF READERS. *Our arrangements have been made without regard to expense. And we encourage the hope that public opinion will pronounce* "THE NEWS OF THE WORLD" *the* BEST, *as well as the* LARGEST *and the* CHEAPEST *of all the Newspapers that are Published.*

We abstain from elaborate introductory observations. The contents of the Broad Sheet now in the hands of the Reader, will manifest our determination to avail ourselves of every means of making "THE NEWS OF THE WORLD" *most useful as a Political Guardian and Guide, and most interesting as a Newspaper to the general Reader. It is only by a very extensive Circulation that the Proprietors can be compensated for the outlay of a Large Capital in this Novel and Original Undertaking; but they are confident that Public Patronage will keep pace with desert, and that the numerous attractions—the intrinsic merits, as well as the extraordinary Cheapness of* "THE NEWS OF THE WORLD" *will be duly appreciated: and that, in point of Circulation this Paper will soon stand first among the most Popular, as no pains will be spared to establish its character as First among the Best of the Weekly Journals.*

WE MOST POSITIVELY AND DISTINCTLY STATE, THAT UPON NO ACCOUNT SHALL ANY ALTERATION EVER BE MADE IN THE PRICE OF "THE NEWS OF THE WORLD." WE INTEND, AND ARE RESOLVED, *that it* SHALL BE SOLD FOR THREEPENCE ONLY. We distinctly pledge ourselves to this. *We enter into an inviolable compact with the Public, never to Charge for* "THE NEWS OF THE WORLD" *more than its present Price. One of the great features of the Publication is its Extraordinary Cheapness; and this great feature shall never be interfered with, on any account whatsoever.*

We are induced to make the above declaration in emphatic terms, on account of the Price of Newspapers having been advanced, by degrees, after a certain Circulation has been

A Few Words of Introduction from the first edition of The News of the World.

People like to keep up with current news. It is said that yesterday's news is 'old news' which nobody wants to read. Is this true? Can old news be of interest? If so, how? and to whom?

Read the 'few words of introduction' from the first *News of the World*. What can you say about the writing style of this piece? Could you rewrite this in the way it might appear in a modern copy? Do you think the paper has achieved its original intentions?

Find out if any of your local newspapers started life in the 19th century. Contact those that did to see if they can send you any information about those early days. They may be prepared to send photocopies of Victorian editions. Your local library may also be able to provide help with this research. What can you learn about life in your area from old newspapers?

Advertising

Advertising really took off in Victorian times. There were more newspapers, more people able to read, and simply more people living in towns and cities with money to spend. Improved communications helped the new manufacturing industries to sell their goods.

The latest in tin baths for those without bathrooms.

MR. CHARLES DICKENS
WILL READ IN THE ROUND ROOM, ROTUNDA, DUBLIN:—
On MONDAY EVENING, AUGUST 23rd, at 8 o'Clock, his
CHRISTMAS CAROL.
On TUESDAY EVENING, AUGUST 24th, at 8 o'Clock, his
CHIMES.
On WEDNESDAY AFTERNOON, AUGUST 25th, at 3 o'Clock, the Story of
LITTLE DOMBEY.
On THURSDAY EVENING, AUGUST 26th, at 8 o'Clock,
THE POOR TRAVELLER,
BOOTS AT THE HOLLY TREE INN AN[illegible] MRS. GAMP.

PLACES FOR EACH READING:—Stalls (numbered and reserved [illegible] shillings; Unr[illegible] Seats, Half-a-Crown; Back Seats, One Shilling.

Tickets to be had of Mess[illegible]. McGlashan and Gill, Publishers, &c., 50, Upper [illegible] Street, Dublin, where a Plan of the Stalls may be seen.

Each Reading will last two hours.

☞ On only one occasion, during Mr. Dickens's experience, some ladies and gentlemen in the Stalls caused great inconvenience and confusion (no doubt, unintentionally), by leaving their places during the last quarter of an hour of the Reading, when the general attention could least bear to be disturbed. This elicited a strong disposition in other parts of the Hall towards an angry but not unreasonable protest.

In case any portion of the company should be under the necessity of leaving before the close of the Reading in the apprehension of losing railway trains, they are respectfully entreated as an act of consideration and courtesy towards the remainder, to avail themselves of the opportunity afforded by the interval between the parts when Mr. Dickens retires for five minutes.

[P. T. O.

A poster for a public reading from his work by Charles Dickens

Judson's Simple Dyes – an example of a punning slogan.

Sunlight Soap – this stamp of approval uses puns and an imaginative image taken from the popular penny post system.

GREAT EASTERN RAILWAY.

BOOKING OFFICES FOR PASSENGERS ARE NOW OPEN AT REGENT CIRCUS, PICCADILLY, AND LUDGATE CIRCUS, FLEET STREET.

Passengers are now Booked at 28, REGENT CIRCUS, PICCADILLY, AND AT Messrs. COOK & SON'S OFFICE, LUDGATE CIRCUS, FLEET STREET

LIVERPOOL STREET & ST. PANCRAS STATIONS, LONDON.

SINGLE JOURNEY TICKETS

RETURN TICKETS

The following are some of the principal places on the Great Eastern Railway:—

TICKETS FOR ROTTERDAM, ANTWERP, And other Parts of the Continent.

S. SWARBRICK, General Manager.

LONDON BRIGHTON AND South Coast Railway, AND THE ISLE OF WIGHT.

IMPORTANT NOTICE.

ISSUE OF TICKETS TO ALL STATIONS ON THE ABOVE LINE, AT Messrs. COOK AND SON'S TOURIST OFFICE, LUDGATE CIRCUS,

Where also information generally as to the Times of the BRIGHTON COMPANY'S TRAINS, &c., May be obtained.

The Fares for Tickets obtained at this Office will be the same as charged at Victoria & London Bridge Stations.

The Tickets will, on issue, be dated to suit the convenience of Passengers.

PULLMAN CARS.

TICKETS FOR PARIS AND THE CONTINENT

The Shortest and Cheapest Route FROM LONDON, Via Newhaven, Dieppe, and Rouen.

(By Order),
J. P. KNIGHT, General Manager.

A page of advertisements in the *Excursionist and Tourist Advertiser* (mid-century) published by Thomas Cook who started a successful travel business which still flourishes today.

Sunlight Dial – a do-it-yourself give-away sundial advertising the soap.

An 1861 bill poster for a popular local theatre in Lambeth where dog dramas with canine heroes were a speciality.

An advertising series of literary figures from Brown and Polson's.

Crane's Black Lead, Servant's Friend series. An early example of a special offer and an encouragement to collect give-away cards.

The innovative hairwasher for the Empire traveller!

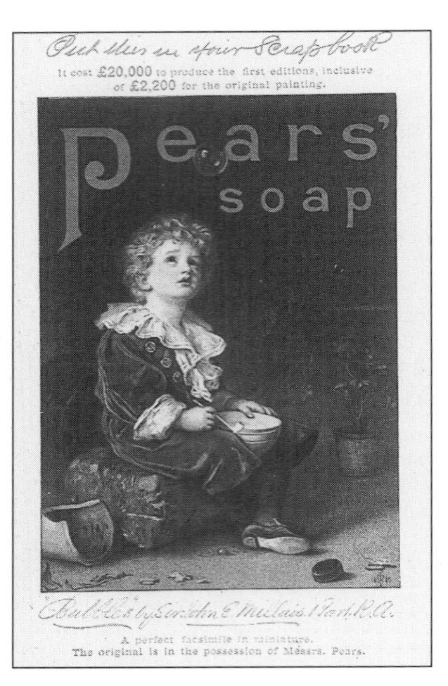

Bubbles – One of the best known advertisements. It uses a painting by the famous Victorian artist, John Everett Millais.

Study the adverts on these pages. Look for the ways in which the advertisers have tried to create interest in what they are offering.

Is there any wordplay involved? Are there any phrases to suggest the things are new/ modern/ effective/easy to use/not to be missed/recommended by anyone/good value? How do they compare with adverts today? Find some adverts for the same sort of things to compare them with. Are they more wordy, or less? What part do pictures/images play? What part do slogans play? What can we learn about an age through its adverts?

Design your own advert for something Victorian. First, decide what you are advertising eg a book, an event, an outing, a theatre bill, or a product. Then, decide whether it will be a poster, in a newspaper, magazine or book, a manufacturer's product board outside a shop, or a give-away with a product.

This advertisement, based on the alphabet, appeared in *The Times* in 1842.

To widowers and single gentlemen

Wanted by a lady, a *situation* to superintend the household and preside at table. She is agreeable, becoming, careful, desirable, English, facetious, generous, honest, industrious, judicious, keen, lively, merry, natty, obedient, philosophic, quiet, regular, sociable, tasteful, useful, vivacious, womanish, xantippish, youthful, zealous, &c.

Try writing your own alphabetical advert. It could be trying to persuade someone to adopt a stray animal or buy a house.